The

LITTLE BLACK BOOK

of

HUMAN RESOURCES
MANAGEMENT

Barry Wolfe

The Expressive Press
www.TheExpressivePress.com

ISBN-13: 978-1515298427
ISBN-10: 1515298426

Books from The Expressive Press

- VB.Net Web Development by Dr. Charles Wood
- By Pete Geissler
  - The Power of Writing Well
  - The Power of Being Articulate
  - The Power of Ethics with Bill O'Rourke
  - The Power of Dignity
  - Divorce can be Such Sweet Sorrow
  - An Accidental Life
  - Hugging A Cloud
  - Bigshots' Bull*!@#

Wolfe, Barry
The Little Black Book of Human Resources Management

1

To my father

Richard Wolfe

My first and best teacher about business, leadership, and the human in human resources.

Table of Contents

Introduction

I'm sure you've noticed that this book is not called *The Complete Guide to Everything You Need to Know to Succeed in Human Resources,* or *The Essential Things You Need to Know About Human Resources.* It does not address every aspect of the profession equally. In fact, it does not address several aspects at all. It does not contain much of the critical information needed to do any job in Human Resources, such as you would learn about in a textbook or college classroom. It certainly does not wax rhapsodic about the *need to* **take the lead** to **transform your organization**, or to fill your working days with *PASSION* for *helping your employees be the BEST THEY CAN BE!* Business publishers' lists are gorged with those books, and some of them are actually worth reading.

So then what is this book about? It's about the stuff you learn when you've worked for a boss you'd swear jumped out of a Dilbert cartoon; worked in a business whose performance careened up and down like a runaway clown car; when you've faced legal or ethical problems that needed the wisdom of Solomon to sort out while they roiled your guts at night; when you've sat on the stand across from some third-rate Perry Mason, or tried to be one yourself.

It's about what you learn when you've knocked yourself out to put measurable six-figure savings back on the company's bottom line; or when an employee pleads for her job with tears in her eyes as she lies through her teeth to your face, or when you've faced down an employee who was spoiling for any chance he could get to sue your organization crippled; or maybe when you've dealt with the employee who told his supervisor he's going to shoot himself.

Like most everyone else, whenever I've cleaned up some HR mess – or made one of my own – I would learn something that I tucked in my back pocket, to pull out as needed when something similar popped up. Some people call this their bag of tricks, or wisdom. I've always thought of it as my little black book.

Practically anybody with 15 or so years' experience could have written this book, and surely some would have done better. I guess I just thought of it first. I can't do much about that, but I hope that a peek through my little black book of HR will spare you, dear reader, a few bloody noses in your HR career, or shave a few degrees off of your learning curve.

So You're In HR...

Tell somebody you work in human resources, and the response is typically an expression of sympathy. "Whoa, man," people will say with a half smile and a gentle, stinks-to-be-you headshake. "You've got to have the worst job in the company!"

How wrong they are. I've been an HR leader for over 20 years, and I still find there is a lot to love about this line of work. For starters, the variety of responsibilities is surprisingly wide. One minute you're doing line-by-line quote comparisons for benefit renewals, the next you're coaching a manager on how to address a performance problem in his area in a way that is fair, consistent with precedent, and doesn't expose the company to legal action.

Then after lunch you're meeting with the company President to discuss the key skills the business will need to support its growth plan, and how you're going to acquire them. On the drive home that night, you're going to shut off the radio and kick around your budding proposal to restructure the work in an area to develop real cross-functional work groups.

That's a pretty cool day, and there's a better than even chance that the next one won't look anything like it. When you're an HR leader, you're a paper shuffler, a number cruncher, a cheerleader, an ethicist, judge, junior lawyer, dean of discipline, father confessor, a visionary, a confidant, and a shaker.

But above all, a good HR leader is a business partner. If you got into this field because you want to stand up for the little guy against the callous forces of impersonal and arbitrary management, you missed your calling, and you should quit and be a community organizer. In a similar vein, you can meet many companies' expectations of an HR leader by shuffling the paperwork and planning the company picnic. In both of those cases, enjoy making $40,000 a year for the rest of your life and gossiping at the water cooler about what you've heard is *really* going on in the executive management meetings.

Every so often somebody writes another article wondering why HR isn't taken seriously in the board room. Here's the real answer: HR is taken seriously when it's run by leaders who understand their business, who understand business, and who deliver solutions to attract, retain, and develop people in ways that help the business meet its goals. So if you or your boss are complaining that "management doesn't care about HR," I suggest you quit whining and start delivering people solutions that help solve the real problems in the business. HR will only be taken seriously when it deserves to be.

When you solve those problems, in ways that actually help people find greater satisfaction in the work they do and the company they work for, that's a real kick. Getting an e-mail from an employee expressing her heartfelt thanks because you helped resolve a dicey, burdensome problem she was having with a co-worker will make your week. Not only is it gratifying to know you've helped someone in a way that few others in the organization could have, but in their own right those problems are also fascinating challenges. They aren't fun, but there is immense satisfaction to be had when you've gathered the facts, weighed the legal issues, the moral concerns, the company precedents, the work histories of those involved, then made your decision, sold the boss on it, carried it out, and know in your guts that you've done the right thing.

Above all, there is nothing like the satisfaction that comes with coming across a great big idea for the company, selling the boss on it, putting it into place, and watching it actually change things for the better.

But of course, HR isn't all fun and glory. In tough times, you may see a bathroom wall proclamation of what you have in common with a vacuum cleaner. Your profession gives you access to all the juiciest secrets of the business, and for some people none is juicier than knowing everybody's salaries. Therein lies what I think is the first unexpected and unpleasant surprise awaiting every new HR leader, especially those who report to the President: The realization that you are not among the highest paid of your peers, and you're not going to be.

HR can earn its place at the table, but it won't be at The Right Hand. Sorry to have to tell you this, but no matter how much the boss values your contribution, you're just not worth as much as the top Finance guy, or the Sales guy, or the Engineering guy, or the Operations guy, and you never will be. And just to rub it in further, you can know the differences exactly. (Take heart, though; you have a good shot at beating out the IT guy and the Purchasing guy.) Some people can develop a real problem with that, and it just eats them alive. Don't let it be you.

Of course I think most people fight off the temptation, but in any case, that's not what's earning you those pitying head shakes. Resolving interpersonal conflicts invariably takes more patience than I care to have, most of all because people spend more effort trying to win you over than they would if they'd just cut the crap and tell you what's really going on. And those secrets I mentioned – about people you work with and respect - often aren't so much juicy as they are ugly, at times involving things like drug and alcohol abuse, sexual harassment, marital infidelity, and sometimes felonies. You're not just in the loop with that stuff; you're usually the person who has to dig into all their gory details, until sometimes you feel like you shouldn't go home until you've taken a shower. Firing people is hard to get used to, though in time you understand deep down that it's the right thing to do (at least, you'd better; if you don't, you're missing a few steps), and at least it's because people deserve it. But planning and carrying out reductions in force, when you're taking out good people who don't deserve to lose their jobs, will often make you sick to your stomach and give you bad dreams.

9

So when I get those reactions to people learning what I do for a living, here's my response: There's a lot more good than bad in HR, but the bad is terrible.

Oh, but look on the bright side: All that crazy stuff gives you the best workplace war stories at parties, second only to the people who work for the FBI or some covert ops organization. And besides, you don't really have the worst job in the company. That distinction belongs to the Quality Manager. A customer can snort and scream at her until the sun goes down, and she has to take it with bowed head bobbing and hands clasped in white-knuckled supplication. If an employee starts up like that with you, you can just fire him.

So you've got nothing to complain about! You want a job where everything is all smiles and roses? Go sell flowers. But if you want a career that will engage your intellect, your wisdom, your energy, and – yes – your heart, in which you can do good for your fellow man and the bottom line, and which still pays pretty darn well, then I don't think you can do much better than human resources management. So tell those people not to waste their pity on you; you've got a great job, and I hope the following thoughts will help you do it even better.

The Not-Really-Changing Persona of HR

For all the competing priorities to satisfy, cranky people to mollify, dicey decisions to make, outsized egos to navigate, tight deadlines to hit, and last-minute extensions to business trips in which you could kick yourself because you *knew* you should have packed an extra pair of socks (again!), being part of an organization's leadership team is really fun. It's exciting to have a part in steering an organization's direction, not least because of the other people on the team. Of course, each member – the Finance guy, the Operations guy, the Sales guy – has a unique role to fill. But when you're the member who's responsible for human resources, if you're going to be successful you have to recognize that you have more than a role to fill. Unlike everybody else who sits around the table at the President's staff meetings, to a certain extent you also have to fulfill a persona.

I'm not talking about conforming to a stereotype. We tease Finance guys for being cold-hearted and withdrawn, Operations guys for being hard-headed, and Sales guys for being affable, shallow, fast talkers. (Don't fear being left out of the fun: We're the touchy-feely wimps, misplaced English majors with no heads for business.) There are lots of people in those roles whose personalities conform to type; but of course there are many who don't, and whether they do or don't has no bearing on whether they're successful. Even the President can be an enlightened humanitarian or an egomaniacal ogre, and still be regarded as good at what he does.

11

But unique among all the positions on the leadership team, the HR leader has no such flexibility. For better or worse, people in every organization, at every level, have expectations about what kind of person you should be, and you can only be so successful if you can't fulfill at least some of them. The organization demands that you be a people person.

Fortunately, that doesn't mean that you have to be a glad-handing social butterfly; but employees do expect that you will be visible, approachable, easy to talk to, fair-minded, and sincerely concerned for their well-being. They want everybody in management to be that way; but the Finance guy can spend most of his career in his office, to be seen only when he shuffles his way through a presentation at an employee meeting, and no one will seriously question his capability to do his job. They just don't look to him to contribute to the organization that way. But if that's how you plan to spend your career in HR, I can promise you that, no matter how clever your incentive compensation plan, no matter how incisive your metrics dashboard, no matter how compliant your employee handbook, the general employee population will not regard you as someone who does what you should be doing.

Once, after starting a new job, I listened to several people discuss my predecessor with sincere, head-shaking disdain. It's not that they thought he was incompetent, or even that he was unfair. The problem was that he stayed in his office and didn't know anyone's names.

People want to trust HR to be the department that looks out for them, that will help them get a fair shake in the organization. That's a worthy reputation for any HR function to aspire to – as long as you don't play too much to "the will of the people" (I mentioned that earlier, and I'll have more about that later). And it pays bigger dividends than how people perceive your department. When HR has that reputation, the entire organization has that reputation.

There's a practical reason for adopting the HR persona, too. Your department is charged with heading off employee problems, and besides all your trainings and your policies, one of the most effective ways you can do that is to be a person to whom people can bring problems. You need people to be able to walk in to your office, close the door, and tell you they think they've been sexually harassed before they tell an attorney, or stop you on the floor to tell you that some of the guys had been to a meeting at the local union hall.

Maybe you have confidence in your fair-mindedness (as I'm sure you should); but maybe cultivating the rest of the HR persona is a bit out of your comfort zone. Don't worry. Like I said, it doesn't demand that you be an extroverted ball of sunshine. To tell you the truth, personality tests I've taken tell me I'd rather socialize with a few friends than go to a big party. That doesn't mean I can't be good at this aspect of my job. It's not a matter of "feeling the part;" It's a matter of adopting some specific behaviors. Here are some that work for me:

1. Learn people's names and use them. Seriously. Keep an employee list on hand and memorize with their pictures if you have to. I don't remember names easily myself, but if I can put this in practice, so can you. Get the names right.
2. Management 101 tells you to get your rear end out of your office. But the HR persona demands more. Make eye contact with as many people as you can; I mean even those 40 feet down the hall, or all the way across the floor. Smile at them, and wave – and when they're in earshot say their names! Do this even if you're in the middle of a hallway conversation. Never let people think you're ignoring them.
3. I said this already, but it's worth saying again: when you're out in the halls or on the floor, smile. Really. But here's a caveat: when you're in the management meetings with your peers or superiors, turn that off or you risk coming off like a grinning lightweight.

You're going to snort at how little these gestures are. Put them to use, and you'll be surprised at how powerful they are. Every other week or so some Big Thinker writes another article talking about The Ever-Changing Role of HR. The HR persona doesn't change.

Writing Policies

When writing employee policies, don't start until you've pasted on the wall the old saying, "hard cases make for bad law." Trying to anticipate all of the situations your policy is meant to cover can conjure up some pretty obscure phantoms, and trying to guard against them would require you to take some steps that really don't apply to the majority of concerns you're facing, for better as well as for worse.

For example, when developing an attendance policy, someone may object to a proposed formulation by saying, "Wait a second! Suppose Bob in Maintenance wakes up and finds out his car won't start? He's a solid guy, but if we had this policy in place, he'd get disciplined!"

Of course you don't want to penalize a good employee needlessly; but how many times has a guy like Bob actually found that his car won't start in the morning? Probably never, because Bob, responsible guy that he is, takes care of his car so that it's ready to go when he needs it. It's the people with attendance problems who also tend to have vehicle problems.

At the other end of the problem scale, some employers will demean their entire workforce to head off some scam that the overwhelming majority of their employees wouldn't dream of trying. My favorite is the requirement to provide a newspaper obituary to be eligible for taking funeral leave. Sure, there may be somebody in such a company willing to claim a relation falsely to get a day or two off work; but are those lost wages really worth requiring everybody else to prove their honesty when they've just lost a family member? That's just crass.

Every rule can be circumvented except the one about death and taxes. Every system can be gamed. Don't make your people or your company jump through dumb procedural hoops just to avoid that handful of bizarre, one-off situations. Write rules that the vast majority of your people can live with, and manage the hard cases as they come. Of course you have to protect yourself against the rare but potentially serious issues like theft or violence, but once you get past the big issues like those, the rest only deserve so much control. You'll find they are rarer than you think they'll be.

*

That last thought probably had you nodding your head at its plain common sense; but there is one policy in your handbook where all that stuff goes out the window, because every other situation it covers really is an unforeseen one-off that can drive you a little bonkers if you don't administer it properly. That policy is bereavement leave.

Nobody has to tell an HR person that contemporary family life can get pretty complicated. If your policy covers leaves for mothers but not aunts, I guarantee you that someone in your company will lose an aunt who raised him for 4 years, and so was *like* a mother to him and so shouldn't he be eligible for funeral leave?

If your policy covers leave for children through blood or legal guardianship, someone has been living with a person for 15 years who just lost a child, and even though your employee wasn't a legal guardian, well, she was *like* a parent. How about her?

Once you start making exceptions for those circumstances, there's no going back until you revise your policy. So save yourself a boatload of headache: figure out what relationships will and will not be eligible for funeral leave, and tell everyone with a one-off exception request to use PTO – no exceptions.

*

I have become a big fan of no-fault attendance policies (recognizing that they can only be no-fault in the age of ADA and FMLA). If you're requiring a doctor's note after so many days' absence, consider this: Why do you care about the reason for an absence? The time is already lost. Your customer will not think it was ok if the resulting missed deadline was for a very good reason. And when that employee went to the doctor for her slip, she put it on the company health plan. So not only are you making employees chase down information that no real value to you, you're paying for it.

Instead of putting yourself in the position of judge over what's a good or a bad reason for an employee to miss work, it's much easier, cheaper, and more adult simply to establish how much unscheduled absenteeism your organization can live with, and track the occurrences.

*

Avoid turning your employee handbook into a detailed procedure manual, in which, for example, you explain how to navigate to a particular page on the company Intranet to find a form. Eventually the IT people will redesign the whole Intranet and you'll never quite get around to updating the handbook to reflect the change. Policy manuals should be about policies.

Working for the President

Working for the President in a company big enough to have an HR leader is unlike working for anybody else, and not just because of his title. Odds are, he got that top job because he's also the sharpest, hardest working guy in the business. In fact, on the whole he's probably sharper than you are. Sure, you might be able to beat him on *Jeopardy!*, but if you were a business competitor he'd probably take your head off (that's why you went into HR). I've found that to be true even of many Presidents who aren't that successful. Almost certainly he has a bigger ego than you do, but that's only because he's earned it.

Business presidents have certain nearly-universal tendencies. They have opinions about everything, and they are not shy about sharing them. They can have an almost knee-jerk contrarian streak, but it's usually because they are more perceptive than everyone around them. And they really, *really* need to get things done. You might be "results-oriented;" Presidents are results-addicted.

A simple declarative sentence can set all of these characteristics off. You can be part of a meeting with the President, and as it's wrapping up someone will say the new white paint on the door trim looks nice. "No, it's really pearl," the boss will say, "and it was a stupid color choice." The vehemence of his opinion will put an uncomfortable smile on everyone's face, because while some of you may have described white as "unattractive," none of you would have described it as "stupid" (and with everything else on your to-do lists you really couldn't care less). But then the boss will say, "For some reason a lot of people put their hands on the corners as they come around, and that color is going to show all the dirty hand prints. If we're not cleaning that trim every other day our customers will think the place looks like a pig sty when they come."

With shrugs and nods, everyone will concede his point. Now that he mentions it, he's right; in fact people hang on that trim and lean in to talk to people in the room, and that color really will show up all those fingerprints – right at eye level, to boot. And while everyone is exchanging glances of admiration for the boss's attention to things everyone else misses (once again), he's on the phone with the maintenance guy telling him to get that color changed before the day is out.

Boom. Done. Next?

That's what the President is like. And if you work for him, he'll expect you to keep up.

The species of President comes in two varieties, genus public and genus private. (When I write of a President in a publicly-held company, I'm talking about the President of a business unit, not the biggest of big guys all the way at the top.) Presidents in public companies are really, really smart, well educated, professional, and scrupulous about following things like company codes of ethics.

They want to make a lot of money, and are more given to enjoying the trappings of success. Maybe they weren't that kind of person at first, but I guess years of working with people who are that kind of person can't help but rub off. One of the reasons many of them want to get things done is because they are ambitious to get to the next level. If you're ambitious too, it's conceivable that you could follow your President in a promotion to a larger business or bigger role, if he likes you well enough. But it's often not quite that simple; he may have to get those kinds of decisions past a raft of people above him.

Presidents in private companies have much more passion – the better word is love - for the actual work of the business (often because they started it). Because they aren't part of a larger organization they have freer rein to shape their culture. This means they can be admirably paternalistic; they can also be ruthless tyrants. Presidents of many private businesses are to their employees and communities the same larger-than-life figures that many corporate CEOs are. They're not just admired; they are figures of legend. They are not rare, and to work for them is a privilege. They probably aren't as well educated as their public counterparts, but they're every bit as sharp. They've learned through the incredible personal and professional risks they've taken to get their business where it is today - risks for which, to be frank, most of their public counterparts simply haven't got the balls.

Now of course, there are leaders of private businesses who are scandalously greedy, just as there are leaders in public companies who are sincerely motivated to do good for employees and for the larger world. But I do think the distinctions I've described apply very much of the time. Safe to say that you can usually distinguish them by a piece of paper they got earlier in life. For the public President, it's an MBA; for the private one, it's a second mortgage.

There is one thing they both having common, though: they tend to have extremely short attention spans – especially for HR issues.

Keeping the Boss's Fingers off the Stove

I think there's something about being the top boss that, every now and then, makes him want to demonstrate to the world that he's the top boss. Unfortunately, at times his idea of a good demonstration is something that can get the business into trouble. When it's an HR related issue, how do you talk the boss back off of the cliff?

The best way I know is to coach him as you would coach any other person; you lay out the choices and the consequences, and show him out the choice he wants to make isn't really going to get him what he wants. For example, I once had a boss who was frustrated with a problem employee and wanted me to just fire him. "He's just taking up way too many people's time," the boss told me through a clenched jaw. I told him, "Ok, you want me to fire him? Sure I'll do it. And you'll feel good about it - for about 30 minutes.

Because that's all the time he's going to need to walk out of here and down to a lawyer's office, where they'll work up a discrimination claim against us. And if you think this is taking up people's time now, wait until I have to start telling them they're going to have to make time to prepare for their depositions, and then court appearances." By the time I was done talking like this, the boss settled down. A few months later we had what we needed to terminate his nemesis. He stopped taking up everyone's time, and although the boss never said anything afterwards, I think he appreciated me steering him in the right direction.

Some years after that I had another boss at a private company who had, shall we say, a wide tolerance for acceptable behavior at the company Christmas party. He was pretty sanguine about the risks he was running, until I explained it to him like this: "If an employee wraps herself around a telephone pole after this party, maybe she wouldn't hold the company liable, but her spouse might. And if you have to pretty much hand over the keys to the business over it, are you going to be ok saying to your partners, 'sure we set the company back two years; but man, wasn't that a great Christmas party?' If you are, fine – tap another keg; but if you're not, then I think we have to put some guidelines in place to protect the business if something happens."

This style isn't for everyone, of course; as with any act of credible leadership, you have to find your own voice. The trick is to paint the picture in terms that show the choices as stark – and obvious.

Now, in their sallies against convention, these guys know the risks perfectly well. They're not children; so why do they need to push the boundaries every now and again? Here I'm going to play armchair psychologist. I think in their relationships with subject matter expert subordinates like the HR guy and the Finance guy, Presidents at times need to display a sort of calculated rebelliousness. Like the little kid who reaches up for the hot stove while looking over his shoulder to see if anyone's noticing, the boss at times wants to be reassured that, if he gets a little impulsive, or a little too far out there, you'll yank his hands away before he burns his fingers. Maybe it is just recklessness; maybe it's a daring that got him where he is. But maybe, every now and then, the boss just needs to see whether he can rely on his team to keep him out of trouble.

Your boss may or may not argue with my psychoanalysis (mine would; he's a contrarian!), but he would definitely agree with the bigger point; your most important job is to support the President. That means delivering the big-picture HR solutions that support the President's business strategy. But don't forget that it also means keeping a close eye on his fingers' proximity to any and all hot stoves.

*

The President needs people on his team whom he can trust, in a sense that is much deeper than your need to trust your subordinates. He's looking for loyalty from his team. Be loyal. Always look for ways to support the President to employees, and what is sometimes harder, to your peers. Sure, you may have a "what's he doing?" conversation behind closed doors with a particularly trusted peer every now and then, but don't make a habit of it. Offer a perspective to people that supports what the boss is trying to accomplish. If people call you a brown-noser behind your back for it, do it anyway. Far better that than for the President to discover you're throwing daggers behind his back. If you can't be loyal, be gone.

*

The best way to have a successful relationship with your boss is to give him what he wants. Once in a while that means giving him not what he says he wants, but what you think he needs. But don't get cocky; there aren't many of those times. Chances are your boss got to be the boss by being right the vast majority of the time, so don't be too quick to second-guess him. Besides, he's the boss.

*

One of my role models for how an HR leader should interact with the company President is Dr. McCoy from the original "Star Trek." Midway through some tense alien confrontation, McCoy would unobtrusively come up to the bridge and lean against a panel just behind Captain Kirk's chair. But he wasn't just caught up in the face-off with the aliens on the forward view screen; McCoy was watching the crew, and the Captain. After the immediate crisis had passed Kirk would go to his quarters. No sooner had he finished a log entry then there would be a buzz at the door, and McCoy would step in. Without so much as a "mind if I sit down," McCoy would sit down and ask whether Kirk had considered all the ramifications of the course of action he was pursuing, or tell Jim he thought the Captain was allowing a personal feeling to affect his judgment, or that he thought Kirk was pushing a particular crewmember too hard.

Kirk always seemed a little irritated with these exchanges (having the fate of the galaxy in your hands probably does that to you); but he understood that if he couldn't justify himself to a trusted advisor, he probably wasn't making the right decision. And both of them understood that part of McCoy's job was to observe how well the captain and crew were accomplishing their mission, and if he had some misgivings about either of those, he couldn't just grouse about them to himself in Sickbay.

As a senior officer, McCoy had an obligation to share his observations and concerns with his boss. Moreover, being a trusted advisor meant that he couldn't wait until his Captain was in a better mood to speak up; McCoy had to present his perspective so that Kirk could use it in his decision. Whether he accepted it or not was up to the Captain; but McCoy's job was to give his boss that option.

Sometimes their exchanges got so heated that Kirk would later apologize. McCoy always accepted with a generous shrug, as though the apology wasn't needed. Similarly, Kirk never once thanked McCoy even when the advice made all the difference, and you never had the sense McCoy needed the thanks. It was all part of the job.

Maybe you're not in a starship, but Dr. McCoy's relationship with Captain Kirk provides an excellent example of how an HR leader needs at times to interact with his boss. Sometimes the business is facing a difficult challenge that puts the President under stress, and that gives rise to an observation or concern on your part. If you think it's something that could help your boss you have to speak up, even if you're worried he won't take it well. I've been there, and yes, on some occasions my boss didn't take it well; but almost invariably, he came by later to say he appreciated that I had spoken up, and that exchange went on to strengthen our relationship.

Of course, we're talking about a TV show. It's hard to tell the boss something he doesn't want to hear, or to challenge a direction he's taking. There's the reluctance to endure a withering tirade, or even the fear that you risk your job. But whether he'll thank you or take you apart for it, as an HR leader you owe your boss your best advice - whether he wants it or not.

*

When you make a mistake, own up; bosses dislike incompetence, but they can respect forthrightness. And they despise cowardice.

*

What the Boss Wants From You

When you start a job in HR leadership, you have a head full of job descriptions and interview forms, of EEO and ERISA compliance requirements, of plans to do supervisor training in employment law, and maybe applying somebody or other's approach to doing good performance appraisals. Oh, what a fine job you'll do! Won't the President of your company be pleased?

Well, I'm sorry to have to be the one to tell you this, but here's a sorry little dose of hard truth: The President of your company doesn't give a crap about 75% of what you do. Don't get me wrong; he knows he needs you. He wouldn't have hired you otherwise. And he'll give you time to talk about what you're doing in his staff meetings. He'll even look at you while you're talking. But if you use the bulk of your face time with the President to talk about the nuts and bolts of HR, you'll start to notice at those times how his face settles into a vacant smile, and how his head starts nodding at odd times, and how he politely thanks you for your input before turning to pull apart what the Operations guy or the Finance guy are telling him. If those sessions leave you feeling self-conscious and miffed at the lack of attention, don't make the fatal mistake of blaming the boss for "not caring about HR." The problem isn't that he doesn't care about your field. The problem is that his HR person isn't giving him what he really wants.

Look, he didn't get his MBA or his second mortgage and commit to 70-hour work weeks so he could administer employee benefits (unless, of course, he's running a business that administers employee benefits). He knows someone has to do it, and he wants it done right, but that's probably not what he's thinking about when he shuts off the car radio on the drive home at night. In fact, if that does have to be the topic for his drive home, he's probably not happy about it, because it's keeping his thoughts from other, more pressing problems – such as the problems he didn't hire people like you to take care of for him.

The psychologist Frederick Herzberg divided factors influencing employee motivation into what he called "hygiene" and "motivation" factors. Hygiene factors don't motivate people, but they create dissatisfaction when they're not present to a satisfactory level. For example, a well-kept office won't make you a happier employee, but if your employer never gets someone to dust your office and empty your trash can, it will probably make you a less happy employee. Motivation factors actually do contribute to job satisfaction when present, like having a boss who recognizes the great work you do. You could divide your responsibilities in the same way. Like other staff-level functions, a lot of HR concerns the things people just expect a business to do correctly, like EEO and ERISA compliance, and supervisor training. He wants you to keep the noise down. Get the administrative work done and done right, so he doesn't hear any complaints about it. If you're a non-union house, keep the union out. If you have a union, keep it as cooperative as possible.

Handle the employee problems, and do what you can to control costs like employee benefits and workers compensation. Those are the "hygiene" factors to your company President. It's important to do those things well, and getting them right will certainly earn you his appreciation; but it won't earn you a place among his inner circle of people he really relies on to help him tackle the big issues of the business. You need to understand his "motivation" factors, and use the bulk of your time to work on them – and make sure that's what you're talking about in the staff meetings.

What "motivates" a President to value the HR person will vary. I have been surprised over the years by how many business Presidents are really supportive of wellness initiatives. I'm not sure if it's because they appreciate the relationship between a healthy lifestyle and health care costs, or if they're just control freaks who like telling others how to live; either way, you can probably make your boss happy by developing a solid wellness program. But there is one thing above all others that he really wants from you. When your company President is turning off his car radio to think about work, chances are very good that he's wrestling with his two perennial issues; how his business

30

is going to respond to threats, and how it's going to take advantage of opportunities. And he knows that he can't tackle either of them unless he's got really good people. Even more importantly, he knows he's got to have good leaders.

There is nothing your boss wants more from you than finding and growing the best leaders you possibly can. Of course I mean finding them on the outside of the organization, but I also mean those on the inside. You need to be continually evaluating leaders in the business – who has potential for a bigger role, who needs help, and who is just not cutting it. There are scads of people out there dying to tell you how to assess and develop leaders, and I'll leave you to sort out and apply their collected wisdom. But there is more to finding good leaders than administering personality tests or conducting sit-down interviews. Let me offer you two thoughts about how an HR leader should contribute to the search.

First, you need always to be actively learning about the people in your organization. Remember what I said about how "Star Trek's" Dr. McCoy would hang out on the bridge in times of crisis, watching how the captain and crew are doing? For some part of your brain, your every interaction with people needs to involve your inner Dr. McCoy. You might think of it as a series of never-ending job interviews, in which you never stop paying attention to patterns in what people say, how they behave, and how they interact, so that you can form an estimation of what they're good at, where they might need help, how well they can do the job, and whether they could play a bigger role. Always work to have a ready answer when your boss asks, "What do you think of so-and-so?"

Second, like finds like. By that I mean good leaders know how to spot good leaders, and good leaders want to work with other good leaders. So if you're going to sort out who is a good leader and who isn't from job candidates, and if you're going to represent your company in a way that will attract good leaders to your organization, you have to be a good leader. If you've never lead anything bigger than your HR department, it's likely to be awhile before you really develop the savvy that good leaders have in themselves and can recognize in others. So go lead something. If your kid is in Cub Scouts, be the Den Leader. Take on a committee in the local food bank. Just get some experience having to get people to do something. That will help you learn what the boss needs, and help give him the one thing above all others he most wants from you.

RIFs and Restructuring

I said earlier that there's more good than bad about HR, but the bad is terrible. Reductions in force are the horrible. No matter how apparent or how urgent the business need to reduce staff, making the decisions that will take groups of people out of the business with little advance warning – even when they are the marginal performers – is the part of this work that really can take a physical or psychological toll on you. No matter how many times you do them, you can still find yourself losing sleep, or losing your appetite. Sometimes I've had bad dreams for weeks after. But don't feel too badly for yourself (or me); after all, when it's all over, unlike a lot of other good people, you still have a job.

And besides, when it has to be done, it has to be done – and your job is to make sure it's done right. Planning and completing a reduction in force is among the most complex responsibilities of any HR leader. There are myriad technical details that have to be addressed – OWBPA postings, severance agreements, the decisional criteria. The notifications have to be coordinated so that all of the managers involved start at the same time, and are delivering the right message. You have to plan for high-drama contingencies, like someone breaking down in tears, or yelling, or coming back to the office with a rifle. And of course, the bad news has to be delivered so as to preserve the dignity of those affected. Get any of that wrong, and your company could face legal action, or come off as heartless, or bumbling – or both – to those affected, to the survivors, or to the community. Your job is to get the organization through that day without giving anyone a cause for legal action, and in a way that's professional and respectful enough to allow your company to keep its good name.

Perhaps surprisingly, HR people do tend to get the event right. But let's face it; for all their complexity, the steps required to complete a reduction in force are things you can tick off a checklist (besides that, legal action is a comparative rarity). The really hard part of a reduction in force concerns the questions around the actual restructuring of the organization – how you're going to get the business past the trauma that is a reduction force and get on with the business of the business. That's the other, real objective of a restructuring – and that's the one where most of the mistakes get made.

When business turns down and managers have to start reducing staff, there are times when companies opt for letting some people go ASAP, and then others when management can figure out more details later. I think this is the worst approach. When things are bad, the best people need reassurance that you're going to remain a viable, stable employer. Reductions that take place in a drip-drip fashion just keep everybody so on edge they spend all their time in panicked tea leaf reading instead of working. The best approach – to use an appropriately ugly metaphor – is to swing the axe once, make a big, bloody mess, and then get the survivors focused on cleaning up and moving on. Maybe that's not possible in all circumstances (though I've had yet to experience them); but the best approach is one tightly planned, well-timed event after which you get all the survivors together and say, "as far as we know, we're done. Let's get back to work."

And you'll know you've done your job when you've made a bloody mess. The longer the deliberation process, the more managers will have back-door meetings with the boss in which they'll plead for their area to be spared, and then your business-saving RIF hinges on taking out the cleaning staff. When business turns south, you just seldom get the numbers where you need them to be without just making a mess.

*

In some RIFs, you'll find the boss wringing his hands most about what to do about one particular guy. He's just not doing the job – maybe he's an impediment to real progress in the organization, or he's just not as aggressive as a guy in his position needs to be. Trouble is, he's been a key guy with the place since the dawn of time, and he knows every part number on every product, or he knows all the players in all the major customers. The boss will say, "He's not doing the job the way we need it done; but man, I just don't know that we can keep the doors open without him."

Trust me: advise him that yes, you can. Maybe that guy has all the knowledge in his head; but if he's not applying it in the rest of the business, it's not doing you any good anyway. I have wrestled that question with bosses on several occasions. Every time we held our breaths and took the guy out, never once –

never once – did we ever regret it. In fact, after those people were gone, customers and employees offered surprising stories from out of the woodwork about how deeply this person had frustrated people inside and outside of the organization.

*

Sometimes, in a fit of "compassion," the boss can ask if there's someplace else you could assign that long-term but failing employee. Take him out. Survivors who are demoted tend to react in one, or both, of two ways; either they just spread poison around, or they become lazy after surviving despite what they know is their substandard performance. What they *won't* be is grateful to still have a job. That's what they'll tell you to your face; but trust me, once their relief at having dodged the bullet wears off that's not what they'll be telling their friends around the water cooler.

And by the way, your company's lawyer may tell you that it's better to keep a disgruntled employee tied somehow to the organization, because it's less likely that person will sue. This is one of those few times (and there really are few) where your lawyer's advice is not usually (that's *usually)* in the best interest of the organization. As I said earlier, you have to get the organization to get past the RIF and get back to work as soon as possible, and demoted survivors tend to stay damaged goods who don't get past it.

*

This need for closure is another reason why I am not a fan of temporary pay reductions as an alternative to a reduction in force. They may be appropriate if you have confidence in the duration of period after which you can restore people to their prior pay levels – say, a key customer will need product at a certain time. But if that time frame is beyond six months I'd wonder how much confidence you can have in your customer's assurances.

Sharing the pain in the interest of keeping all employees working seems like the compassionate, team-spirited thing to do. But pay reductions of more than just a few months – like, three – tend to have most people feeling less and less of that 'ol team spirit. Before long spreading the pain just becomes spreading the poison.

The other problem is that your A players, who are critical to getting you through the downturn, can't help but start questioning your viability as an employer. For their sakes, the rest of your employees, your customers, and the community of which you're a part, any organization is far better off projecting an image of being a smaller but healthy operation than limping along as a larger but sicker one.

Details of RIFs are often the most closely guarded secrets in a business (except for that bonehead on the staff – often the Sales guy - who can't help showing off to his people how in the know he is). That's entirely appropriate; everybody knows when a RIF is coming, and the anticipation sets people so terribly on edge that that's when the rumor mill can do some of its wickedest work. But at some point in the days leading up to the event, you may find yourself in a hallway conversation, or taking questions at an employee meeting, and somebody will look you straight in the eye, and with a slight quiver in her voice, ask you, "is there going to be a layoff?"

Before you think about how you'd answer, remember this. While you and your peers have been squirreled away in the conference room deciding who's on The List and who isn't, the rest of the employees have been lying awake nights wondering how in God's name they're going to make ends meet if they lose their jobs.

Now, the confirmation that a layoff is imminent can spur some people to some unsavory steps in what they think will save their jobs. Some people will have "an injury." Some people will raise an allegation of unethical behavior to gain whistleblower protection. Some people may figure their number is up, and do some act of sabotage in revenge. Be careful about those contingencies.

But there is an even more important consideration. A company's ability to survive a RIF demands people's trust in management.

And people look to the Human Resources leader as the organization's embodiment of integrity, in many cases to a degree even greater than they do the President. So this is not the time for you to give one of those mealy-mouthed lawyerly BS answers that start with, "well, we're weighing all of the options and we continue to evaluate them in light of what's best for the viability of the organization in the long term…"

For God's sake, don't give them that crap at a time like that. And if you're going to lie and say the decision hasn't been made when it pretty well has, go get another job, because you've just forfeit your credibility. In spite of all the risks, if someone is asking you that straight-up question, there's only one answer you can give: "I'm sorry, but yes there is."

Training

Picking a third party to deliver your leadership training is one of the most critical decisions an HR leader can make. It's not so much because they hold the key to your business' future, but because you'll only figure out whether you've made a good choice after your organization has shelled out huge bucks and sucked up gobs of your key people's time in classrooms. If you're going to make leadership training an effective investment for your organization, here are a few things you should keep in mind.

Training consultants want to think of themselves as experts whose cellophane-wrapped 4-color binders are going to turn your sleepy-eyed supervisors into Julius Caesars. They won't, at least not on their own.

Training is not magic pixie dust. You can buy magic pixie at Walt Disney World – it's got Tinker Bell's picture on it. But you know what? It's still stamped tin foil. If even Walt Disney can't make real magic pixie dust, neither can training providers. I'll bet you know that; I'll also bet your senior leadership hasn't much thought about it.

The decision to deliver leadership training is only one of two necessary decisions a business makes. The second is how your business is going to support the content that the trainer delivers. Those experts know what's in their binders, but they don't know your business. That means your senior leaders –

not just you - need to rip that cellophane off some of those binders and decide how the content is going to be supported after it has been delivered. And if senior leadership isn't going to do things the way the training materials say to do it, then you need either to get another training provider or start taking pages out of the binders, and the self-proclaimed experts be damned.

They all say, "We listen to our clients. We're not hammer salesman, who tell clients that the solution to all of their problems is a hammer." Then they proceed to sell you a hammer, because hammers are still what they sell. Leadership training is often necessary, but often your organization really needs is leadership development. Don't start advocating either until you're sure of the difference and which your organization actually needs, or you'll risk making a very costly and credibility-damaging mistake.

*

Barry's Laws

Besides suitability of the content to your organization, and your senior leadership's commitment to reinforcing the content once delivered, the other issue is just efficacy of the content, i.e., whether the content transfers into actual behavior changes outside of the classroom. You can work through the mountain range of theorizing on this topic at your leisure, but as a primer I'd like to offer Barry's Two Laws of Skill Transference:

1) The true is not as important as the useful, and

2) The useful always stands in inverse proportion to the amount of geometry used.

Let's start with that first one. A lot of leadership training programs devote time to teaching theories of motivation. Fine; good idea. If you help managers develop an understanding of why people do what they do, those managers can apply that understanding to help people become more effective on the job. But introducing a theory all by itself, even the one regarded by your training provider as The One, or as true, isn't necessarily helpful if it doesn't present clear, simple ways to apply it. For example, Freud's construct of consciousness as id, ego, and super-ego may be "true;" but if applying that theory meant your shop supervisor would have to respond to an employee's failure to wear her safety glasses by scheduling hourly sessions each week for six months to discuss why she hates her mother, I doubt your employer (or that supervisor) would consider all that to be a worthwhile investment of time. Fortunately for all concerned, Freud's model isn't really considered "true" these days. But even if it were, it wouldn't be worth teaching in a leadership training program, because it doesn't give leaders useful approaches to addressing employee problems or building a high performance team.

To use a more substantive example: In my humble opinion, I think Vroom's revised theory of expectancy is really on to something, but I would never present it to a group of managers and supervisors. For people who have other things to think about - like how the business will make the money that pays my salary - it takes too long to explain, and once it is explained, how to apply it just isn't that obvious.   True is good; useful is better.

So how can you tell that a topic, even if true, will be useful to an audience? That's where Barry's Second Law can be a guide. I've sat through my share of approaches to leadership training, and I've found that a concept that's likely too complex to be generally applied is presented with some chart or slide with text in boxes inside circles and arrows pointing all over the place. An iterative process represented by text boxes connected by arrows going around in a circle is pretty easy to convey. So is a sequential concept with text boxes pointing from one to another.

A 4-quadrant graph isn't too bad, but make that explanation quick. But the circle of text surrounded by boxes and a wavy line that looks like a double helix with the description in bold and…well, I'm sure it got someone their PhD, but it's just not likely to be the tool that helps managers lead their people more effectively. The more geometry it takes for an instructor to convey a concept, the less likely that concept will see any application in the real world.

Here I'm going to single out an example that will likely turn into a bit of a rant. Ask business leaders about theorists of human motivation they've heard of, and most probably couldn't identify MacGregor, or Taylor, or Herzberg, or

Vroom. But most, if not all, have heard of Abraham Maslow and seen his pyramid called the Hierarchy of Needs. If you're fortunate enough not to have encountered it, I'm not going to waste your time here explaining it; it's easy enough to find on the Internet. For the life of me, I cannot understand why trainers still resort to that snake oil on a wall chart. If you see it in some peddler's four-color binder, close it up, hand it back to him, and say thanks very much, but you're looking for material developed by people with something actually worth teaching.

In the first place it obviously explains nothing about human motivation on Planet Earth. Mother Theresa and Mahatma Gandhi were probably two of the most self-actualized people of all time, and let's just say neither of them devoted a lot of effort to meeting their physiological or security needs. In fact, they probably would have said that was exactly why they achieved their self-actualization.

Not only is Maslow's Hierarchy not true; it also isn't useful. I have helped managers deal with eleventy hundred or so employee problems, and in listening to their analysis of an employee issue, never once – never *once* (do you understand that I mean not a single time?) – have I heard one of them say, "… and then Maslow's Hierarchy of Needs came to mind, and I thought, 'wait a minute! It's obvious that her unfulfilled material needs are inhibiting her ability to achieve self-actualization. No wonder she's not coming to work on time!'" I'm going to go out on a limb here and say the same is true for you, too. Even if a trainer actually believes the pyramid to be true, no one has ever plausibly explained what he or she expects a manager to do with it.

As for the geometry, the problem isn't that a stacked pyramid is too complex; it's just that even its proponents acknowledge so many exceptions to it that it long ago stopped even representing the theory.

So if you want to train managers about motivation, I'd rather just tell them that behavior is a function of its consequences; why people do something depends on what happens when they do it. Someone once observed that concept is almost Pavolvian. Maybe it is; but so what? You don't need a wall chart of encircled rhombuses to explain it, it's easy to apply, and it will get your managers through about 80% of all the leadership challenges they'll ever encounter. As for that other 20% – well, that's another reason they've got you around.

*

When managers are talking shop after hours and the HR leader isn't around, I suspect a lot of them go on about how they'd just strap on their metaphorical six-shooters and go rid the Dodge City that is their department of its malcontents and underperformers, if it weren't for that bureaucratic wimp Sherriff HR Leader and all his wimpy talk about "policy" and "fairness" and "the law."

That's probably true for a certain number of them (especially most business Presidents or Operations guys, who are generally not the most patient individuals); but if they went over to the table where the HR people are gathered, they'd hear stories of HR leaders having to drag managers out into that street, pin their tin stars on their chests, and force the gun into their uncertain and shaking hands.

Why are so many managers so reluctant to confront their own problem employees? Sometimes it's because they're the wimps. It may also be because you haven't created a clear policy manual and performance coaching process (in which case put down your drink and get back to work!). But more often than not, it's because those managers just don't know their ground. They go to work every day with their heads filled with those lunatic headlines about colossal employment-related settlements, and if they don't understand the legal environment in which they're leading people, they can be afraid to insist on a deadline being met for fear of provoking a lawsuit that will cost them their jobs or land them in jail. That's where I think training in employment law goes a long way.

Too often, we train managers in harassment or discrimination in the interest of avoiding a problem – we do it because we don't want them to screw something up (and let's face it; it's often done so that the company can distance itself from the manager who does screw up). But if we give them a broader grounding in the employment law landscape, we're helping them find the confidence they need to reach for their stars and send their ornery miscreants a-packin'.

Performance Appraisals

To Appraise or Not to Appraise

In the past several years some people have argued vehemently against performance appraisals. In some cases "vehemently" is too weak a word; a better choice might be "rabidly." It's true that no less a figure than W. Edwards Deming said they're a complete waste of time; but to read what some of today's Big Thinkers say about them, you'd think that performance appraisals are reducing employees and managers to quivering lumps of traumatized blubber. "Surveys show that employees and managers alike HATE them!" (I wonder what surveys show about employees and managers' attitudes towards filling out purchasing requisitions.) "NOTHING creates greater anxiety in organizations than performance appraisals!" (Really? Ever been through an acquisition?) "Get rid of them before they DESTROY YOUR COMPANY CULTURE!" My goodness, is this a management process or an invasion from outer space?

Well, once we've finished breathing into the brown paper bag, I'd like to disagree. Granted, making quantifications and comparisons about an abstraction like performance is, shall we say, inherently problematic. That reality would be easier to accept if it weren't often so terribly consequential to people's careers. Any manager who takes it seriously will say it's among the most difficult of her responsibilities.

But people need to know how they're doing. Successful performers need to be confirmed in what they're doing right so they continue doing it. Less than successful performers need to understand the gap between what they're delivering and the company's expectations. Everyone wants the good opinion of his or her employer. Whether they're willing to do what it takes to earn it is a different question; but at the very least, people deserve to know whether they have it or they don't. This is where the abolitionists cry, "but feedback needs to be ongoing and real time!" True enough; but most every person working out here on Planet Earth will tell the abolitionists that that hardly ever happens.

And employees aren't the only ones needing this information. Organizations need to know who gets promoted and who stays in place, who gets the big raise and who gets no raise, who stays and who goes. The company's leaders must provide those answers, and just because that's not popular doesn't mean it isn't necessary. Until the hyperventilating Big Thinkers can tell us how to address those needs, I don't know how else to do it other than with a well-designed performance appraisal instrument supported by solid training.

Who exactly is doing all this trembling and hand-wringing about performance appraisals, anyway? I don't hear it from the A players (unless they're subject to the judgment of a B or C player manager, in which case the issue is a problem of management, not the appraisal process). In truth it's usually left for the B and C players, who don't like to be confirmed in their mediocrity. In today's hyper-egalitarian, everyone-is-special world, it's pretty jarring for some people to realize that delivering "acceptable" work with minimal effort year after year doesn't result in big raises. But with that said, for all the moaning and hand-wringing on the part of some managers, most people sincerely appreciate receiving a thoughtful, candid, professionally delivered performance appraisal – even when it's other than enthusiastic.

I think the principal objection to performance appraisals is a matter of babies and bathwater. So many appraisal instruments are little more than lists of performance dimensions with no more definition to them than their associated grading scales. The lack of clarity can result in some conversations that, to someone listening in, can sound more than a little silly. "Gee, Mary, I got all that tough work done on time two months ago! I'd say I'm a 4 for Commitment." "I know Hal, but you got this other stuff late. I'd say that's 3." So Mary has to decide whether Hal "is one number or another," and for a performance dimension that requires her to look inside his head. With so little guidance to make such consequential decisions, no wonder people get a little agitated.

Plenty of businesses suffer under poorly designed and implemented appraisal processes, but in concept and practice, there's little inherently wrong with them that couldn't be fixed. You need thoughtfully designed instruments that align with the company's expectations and identified training needs, a process integrated with decent performance management processes, and managers trained in good performance management principles, who put their big-kid pants on and deliver the honest truth.

Now, if you or your organization isn't willing to put in the effort required to deliver a solid process, that's when I say don't do it at all. When the appraisal instruments don't match the job, or don't help managers distill what they've observed into a coherent and reasoned judgment on how an employee is performing, thus giving the dissatisfied employee all the material she needs to blow the manager's feebly constructed message to bits – *that's* when you get hand-wringing anxiety and a complete waste of time. In fact it's worse than doing nothing.

Badly done appraisals are dangerous things with which to stuff employee files. An employment lawyer I know who defends employers once told me that in fully half the cases she's handled in which performance appraisals were material, the appraisals hurt the case. Either they show a glowing record when the employer is trying to justify a termination for incompetence, or they contain brainless comments that can substantiate claims of unlawful bias. Instead of being the weights that tip the balance of the decision in the employer's favor, these appraisals are indefensible millstones that sink the case.

It is not wrong for a company to make clear to an employee that he or she isn't cutting it, even if that message generates anxiety. The real challenge HR leaders need to address in their performance appraisal process is to help managers show employees how to succeed – to assist an employee in recognizing the problem, develop an effective plan to correct the problem, and follow through on executing the plan. Do those things, and maybe everyone could put their paper bags away.

*

I'm going to start this off with a bit of a rant. A few paragraphs ago, I almost let myself get away with leaving you one of the lamest techniques that plagues people like you and me who read HR's Big Thinkers. Look for guidance on how to construct a good performance appraisal instrument, and most of what you come across are articles with titles like "The Six Big Errors in Performance Appraisals," or "Don't Let These Mistakes Sink Your Performance Appraisal Process." The easiest way for someone to gin up a publishable article on any given topic with the least amount of effort is to remind the world what not to do. (Do the same search on pay for performance and you'll get identical results.) I guess those articles get their authors noticed, but that's about the only purpose they serve. We're looking for solutions; Big Thinkers who seek attention by holding up their "Avoid This!" articles as actually helpful are doing no more service than selling snake oil. And throwing in some dumb platitude about the obvious doesn't make their concoction any more valuable.

Did I really expand your knowledge three paragraphs back by telling you that you need "thoughtfully designed appraisal instruments?" Please.

So now I hope to redeem myself in your eyes by explaining what I think is the best approach to developing a good performance appraisal instrument. It's mostly a synthesis of different examples and different thoughts I've scooped up, but there are some contributions I've made after years of trial and error.

First, you need to identify your performance factors. The best way to work that out is to find the common dimensions by grouping all of your jobs into logical strata. I generally like three - for example, Operative (your direct producers/service providers), Administrative/Professional, and Leadership employees. Yes, appraising administrative and professional employees with the same criteria is a problematic grouping, but in my judgment the difference between three and four levels is too complex an alternative, especially for smaller organizations. Each stratum can have many factors, but each level should have the same number of factors.

I like a five-point rating scale for each factor because it offers the best balance between simplicity in the system and an opportunity to make meaningful distinctions in performance. In addition, it best correlates to the bell curve, which is still the most useful way to conceptualize performance, so useful that whether it's empirically true isn't worth fussing about. People can *get it.* (Notice that it satisfies both of Barry's Laws of Leadership Training!)

I think most of the controversy around the validity and usefulness of the bell curve comes from a lack of recognition that there are two ways to think about a normal distribution, which don't necessarily overlap. We can generally accept that, if you plot the performance of a sufficiently sized group of people, the *quantitative* distribution will be a bell curve. But whether the performance is *qualitatively* identical is a question of your standards.

Now, before we go further, here's my take on how to apply the concept of the bell curve at the level of performance factors. The apex of the curve is, of course, the "3" rating, the far ends of the curve are the "5" (best) and "1" (worst), and midway between the ends and the apex are the respective "4" and "2." The "3" rating is the average quality of performance from the standpoint of a numerical distribution; however, that does not translate to an "average" level of performance – or at least, it had better not.

Since most employees should be achieving your organization's standards, "3" should be the standard of performance to be successful on the job. That's why I don't think "3" should translate into "Meets Expectations" any more than it should "Average:" "Fully Successful" should be the appropriate translation. It means that, in this regard, the employee is doing the job the way it should be done. Not only is it more accurate, it removes the stigma that "3" often carries in employees' minds that their performance is not valued. It also lessens the pressure many managers feel to pad an employee's ratings to avoid demoralizing him or her.

The "4" rating means "Exceeds Expectations." This is the rating for employees whose work in a particular aspect of performance is truly a cut above. "2" means "Does Not Meet Expectations." A manager who gives this rating should be expected to follow up the appraisal with some kind of corrective coaching to close the gap between the company's expectations and the employee's performance.

Your managers should think of the "5" ("Outstanding") and the "1" ("Immediate Improvement Required") as being reserved for the top and bottom 2%. Of course, they won't know the actual distribution of such ratings; but they should understand that those two ratings are at the extreme ends of the spectrum because they are to be used only sparingly. Rating someone a "5" should mean that the person's performance is what you'd see a level or two above them, or rarely exhibited to this degree in the business. It could also mean a person has achieved the "4" results despite some particularly difficult circumstances. A "1" means the performance is so unacceptable as to jeopardize the person's continued tenure with the business if left uncorrected.

Managers should think of "5" and "1" as signal flares sent to upper management, that call attention either to exceptional or seriously problematic performers. Those ratings will attract attention in one-over reviews, so managers had better not be shooting them off without good reason.

With that understanding of the bell curve in mind, let's turn to designing the appraisal instrument. Determining the appropriate performance factors for jobs in your organization takes real, careful thought. Job Knowledge, Quality of Work, and Quantity of Work are pretty popular, for starters. Your businesses' key metrics and behavioral or leadership competencies, if you have them, are good places to start. I wouldn't use more than ten; in fact, I've found that nine about does it.

Whatever factors you settle on, you can't just draw a line for the rating next to each one and start passing out the form. That's how managers and employees end up in those absurd arguments about "being a 4" versus "being a 3" with no common frame of reference to justify their respective positions (in discussions which are supposed to be about performance and not numbers, lest we forget). You have to provide that common frame of reference, and you do it by giving an explanation of each rating for each factor.

A useful rating definition conforms to two criteria: One, it is based on evidence that you can perceive with your eyes or ears (a behavior), touch with your hand (a tangible result), or find on the bottom line (a quantifiable result). Two, it translates into something of measurable value to the organization.

I once came across a rating definition for a Customer Service performance factor, which read "remains cognizant of company standards when interacting with customers." This is perfectly awful for two reasons. For one, it requires a manager to be a mind reader, which is not on anyone's job description because it's impossible. For another, who cares what an employee is or isn't cognizant of? Employees aren't paid for what they think; they're paid for what they deliver. Suppose an employee gets a low rating for Customer Service because he lost his temper with a customer. "But," says the human volcano, "I knew I was violating the company's guidelines on customer service the entire time, so I met the standard!" Maybe he deserves anger management training; but according to the appraisal, he also deserves a 3 for Customer Service (Nice job on the form, HR).

Similarly, I don't like definitions or descriptions of performance factors that begin, "Ability to..." My daughter has the talent to be a very fine piano player, but she didn't practice enough and ultimately gave up the instrument. So, whatever her ability, I can't say my daughter is a good piano player (though I still love her like crazy!).

Performance appraisals are not assessments of abilities; they are assessments of the application of one's abilities. They're not about what one *could* do, but about what one *did* do.

So with all that in mind, let's construct a performance factor. Job Knowledge is pretty popular, so let's go with that. The first step is to develop a definition of what we want to appraise when we use the term "job knowledge." But right off the bat, we should notice that this factor poses two questions: how are we going to appraise what's in an employee's head? And, why do we want to appraise what's in an employee's head? We could answer the first question by giving tests; but not only would that be a time-consuming pain, it wouldn't address the second question. Employers shouldn't value the mere possession of job knowledge; we should value its application. So here's what I'd consider a good definition of the performance factor: "Applies appropriate knowledge for job requirements."

Next, we want to define the ratings – what we mean when we rate someone a 2, or a 4. Ideally, the place to start is at the 3 rating, or to define what is "Fully Successful;" but I have to tell you that this is the single hardest intellectual exercise I've ever undertaken in my HR career, so if a good definition for a different rating comes to mind, then by all means, start there.

Keep in mind that we want to be able to appraise the application of job knowledge with observable, verifiable evidence. So, what might we consider as evidence that someone has the knowledge she needs to do the job? How about this: If an employee knows what she needs to know, she's able to do the job without making a lot of mistakes, or having to ask a lot of questions, or do a lot of research. You can see or hold mistakes, or find them on the bottom line; you can see or hear an employee asking questions, or looking up answers.   So a good definition of fully successful performance would be something like, "Fulfills all job expectations with minimal errors and requiring minimal questions of co-workers." If she's able to get her job done right without having to ask help from co-workers, that's good evidence that she has the job knowledge the organization is looking for.

Continuing in the same vein, here's how all five rating definitions might look:

5 – Has been published in a recognized professional publication; has taken the leading role in developing training materials; or is the recognized "go to guy" for a technical subject (not a business process).

Having more than one type of acceptable evidence for a rating is a good way to help people earn it. Still, there shouldn't be many of these in your organization, but that's as it should be. Remember, 5s are for your top 2% in a given factor. But before you just go pasting this definition into all of your performance appraisals, think through its applicability to all levels in your organization. If a particular Engineer is the only one of his discipline in the organization, does he get this rating not so much by performance as by default? The answer may well be yes, if you think about it; but I'd push back on that reasoning for people at the top like the HR leader. You're being paid to be the go-to person.

4 – Frequently answers questions from co-workers and subordinates and/or delivered at least one training session in past year.

This rating is for the person who is making the extra effort to share his knowledge with others in the organization.

3 – Fulfills all job expectations requiring minimal questions of co-workers.

We discussed this before. Helping new employees get acclimated is still likely within bounds of this rating.

2 – Requires frequent or repeated direction from managers or co-workers to fulfill job expectations.

If an employee is requiring a lot of help from others to get the job done, that's an indication that the manager needs some type of intervention. Of course, this may not be a fair rating for the new person who couldn't be expected to perform otherwise.

1 - Requires frequent or repeated direction from managers or co-workers to fulfill job expectations after having received additional re-training.

This rating tells the employee, "you've had a problem understanding the job, we've invested additional resources to help you, and you're still not getting it. If you can't fix this, your job is on the line."

Not every job deserves an equal chance to earn the top score for every performance factor. The opportunity for a 5 rating in the Job Knowledge factor makes no sense for the guy who mops the floors at night. So on some appraisals, some factors shouldn't even have a "5" rating on the form. If management can't envision what it considers superior performance in a certain job, leaving a "5" rating on for the sake of symmetry on the form is pretty brainless.

Notice that each of these definitions are based on evidence, but not metrics. They don't require the manager to track the number of job-related questions each subordinate asks, with a scale for how many questions become "frequent," or some similar worthless exercise. What this approach does require is that managers pay attention to what their people are doing and to apply good judgment. That's what employees deserve. It's also as much as employees have a right to insist upon.

If slogging through definitions for every rating for every performance factor for every performance appraisal sounds hard, take it from me: it is. The only advice I can give you about how to do it effectively is to write a draft of all of them yourself before you form a committee to review them; trying to get a group to produce these from scratch just isn't a productive use of everyone's time. But the effort pays huge benefits. It allows managers and employees substantively to discuss the realities of what is and what isn't being done, and what really matters, instead of arguing about how to quantify abstractions like performance.

Clear definitions of the grades of performance for a given factor reduce the urge for managers to pad ratings. And when you've done all the hard thinking up front, training managers on appraising performance takes a lot less effort. Best of all, though, this approach helps employees be successful by clearly showing them what the organization values.

Once you've grouped your jobs into classifications that will use similar appraisal forms, and defined your performance factors and ratings, there is one more step. Not every performance factor will have the same importance for every job, even for those using the same appraisal. So develop a standard scale for weighting the different factors. Don't slice the weights too finely; if I'm using nine factors for a performance appraisal, I like weighting two factors at a three, one factor at a one, and the remaining five at a two. Allow managers to weight the factors any way they consider appropriate, so long as they are the same for every employee with the same job title.

To complete the appraisal form, managers multiply the factor weight times their rating for the factor to get a factor score, and total the factor scores for the appraisal score. Then once you're done flogging all your managers to get them done on time, you have one last step: a one-over review.

Its goal is to normalize the scores as much as possible across the organization. You want every employee in his or her proper place on the bell curve. In many companies, a manager's manager does a review of the performance appraisals he has completed to ensure they are being done consistently across the organization. I recommend that be done at as high a level in the organization as is practical, and with senior HR involvement, so that the organization can both get as broad a view of the scoring process as possible, and to communicate to managers as broad a view as possible of how the organization views different performance factors and rating definitions. Even after training, managers of goodwill can still rate their people too low or too high compared to their peers, and contrary to the organization's intent. One-over reviews are an organizational gut check.

When you're conducting one-over reviews, focus mainly on those scored at the ends of the bell curve. Probe managers for the evidence they used to give those 5s or 2s. Is this what the company had in mind? Is it consistent with what managers' peers are doing? You don't have to go through every single person, but it doesn't hurt, especially in the early years of using this process.

So you're probably wondering: What do I with all these scores? The answer – figure out raises, of course! Now you know where I stand on that other great HR controversy about performance appraisals, whether they should be used solely for developmental purposes or also be tied to compensation decisions. I suspect that the only reason people started advancing the opposing argument in the first place is another byproduct of poorly designed appraisal instruments, which generate more heat in the form of arguments between managers and employees than light in the form of thoughtful feedback on performance. Besides, regardless of whether a company has articulated a philosophy of pay-for-performance or not, both management and employees tacitly believe that the more one contributes, the more one should earn.

So if you're not going to give increases on the basis of performance, on what basis will you do it? Try spreading raises like peanut butter, the same for everyone – that gets you satisfied mediocrities and insulted stars. If that's not acceptable, you're back to paying for performance; and I know no better way to do that than to base it off on a well-designed appraisal process.

Paying For Performance

(Reader Discretion Advised)

I'm now going to show you how I turn the results from the performance appraisal process described above into pay increases for employees. But I have to preface this with a warning: The preceding discussion of performance appraisals may have left you nodding your head. The following discussion of what I've found to be the best way to pay for performance may cause you to throw this book against the wall, so you might want to take a deep breath before proceeding (especially if you're reading this in an e-format).

Let me start by saying this: Just as every system can be gamed, so too does every management process have pluses and minuses. The challenge for management is to use a process in which the pluses outweigh the minuses, and then to figure out how best to minimize those minuses.

I came up with the approach I'm going to describe on my own. As you read about it, I have no doubt that you'll find what you consider to be minuses. I'll bet I'd even agree with your points; I simply believe that those minuses do not outweigh its pluses.

This process allows managers to create meaningful distinctions in pay based on performance with a limited increase in budget (which is what most people have had for the past several years, and likely will continue to have); and it provides a straightforward, easily explainable rationale for determining increases that is difficult for employees to argue with. I'd say those are pretty good strengths.

However, it's based on the following premise: Annual increases should be determined by a centralized process, not by individual managers.

If I make that assertion for two reasons; the first is the best interests of the business confronts the reality of limited resources. As we all know, the annual compensation budget is like a pie, which the corporation places on the table and expects various managers to divvy up for their people on the basis of their contribution to the business. It's a zero-sum proposition: High performers get bigger slices of pie than low performers. Now, managers can argue that their star performers deserve really big slices, and senior management could agree with every one of their arguments; but no matter what size of slice someone really deserves, the fact remains that there is still only so much pie to go around.

That being the case, the most desirable outcome for the business as a whole is not for the star in Accounting to get one sized slice and a comparable performer in Shipping to receive a different one; rather, the corporation should want the best performers across the business to receive comparable increases - not identical, but proportionate according to some consistent rationale.

The second reason why I favor a centralized process is that the typical compensation budgeting process can't reward many strong performers in the way the company would like. Many companies start with a corporate increase in budget, which they pass on to managers to divvy up among their people in proportion to their group's headcount. A percentage is pretty common; if the overall budget is 3%, every manager has 3% to spend. Within some kind of guidelines, good performers will get more, and weaker performers will get less.

Now, if you're running a group of 50 people, it's possible to give your strong performers some fairly nice raises; your top one or two can get 5%, and your bottom one or two will get 1%, or some such number. But what if you're running a department of eight people? If you're doing your job, you don't have slackers in your group who deserve 1% increases. So how do you reward your best performers? Most likely, you'll have to do it pretty much the way you'll reward your weaker performers. Everyone will get around the same increase. You may have a star in your group of eight who is just as valuable to the organization as one of those in the group of 50; but your star can't get a 5% bump for no other reason than the size of the group in which he works.

I think that one reason why companies do that is because of a belief in the principle that, within guidelines, managers should have the ability to determine the rewards of their people. That sounds reasonable on the surface. But ability to pay is already the biggest constraint on an organization's capability to reward talent; to divide up that capability even further only increases the constraint. So ultimately, it comes down to rewarding employees competitively versus maintaining a management prerogative. Which of the two will result in the greater increase in shareholder value?

Here's the process I've developed to achieve the first goal. Once you've finished normalizing all of your performance appraisal scores, use MS Excel to group them into five groups of such sizes that you can plot the count of each group as a line graph that will give you a bell curve. If you don't know how to do that, Excel's Help function chart can step you through the process. This can take a fair amount of trial and error to find the cutoffs between groups that will yield a valid curve, but keep at it.

Once you have your groups, build a little table in the upper left hand of your worksheet. Each row in this table shows the score range for a group, the total salaries in the group, the proposed increase percentage, and the increase amount (% increase*salaries in the group). Then total all those proposed increases and subtract that number from your total budget amount to see if you're above or below where you need to be. You can play around with the increase percentages for each group so that you get as close to your budget number as you want (you may want to hold some of that budget back to give out as spot increases during the course of your budget year).

Then just let managers know who is getting what increase, and we'll see you next year!

You may have inferred that the cutoffs between groups can appear rather arbitrary; you might get 68 as the top score for a group one year, and the next it could be 64. It's not arbitrary at all; it's the result of how the distribution of scores for a given year fit the model.

Now, before you go waving this in front of your company's President as the next great HR initiative you have to adopt, one key consideration is the size of your organization. I'm not statistician/behavioral scientist enough to speak authoritatively on this, but it takes a critical mass of employees to represent qualitative differences between employees on a useful bell curve. If management is doing a reasonable job of hiring and performance management, I just don't think a group of 20 will have a number of useless schleps comparable to real standouts that would justify substantial disparities in compensation increases.

Sure, on a 3% merit budget the stars might be worth 5%; but does that mean the worst performers really deserve 1%? After trying this process in various situations, I'd say you need at least a group of 50 to make it work effectively, and for groups larger than 750 it starts getting tough – it's just hard for any one to three people to oversee normalizing performance scores for groups larger than that. For organizations of 1000 or more employees I think it would make more sense to develop curves for groups of employees.

I mentioned earlier that I don't agree with those who argue that the performance appraisal process should be separated from compensation decisions; as you can tell, I think they should be very tightly integrated. But for those who choose to maintain the opposite position, I'd think they would find this process very attractive. It maintains the relationship between performance appraisal and compensation; but it removes the responsibility for the compensation decision from the manager.

I described earlier what I think are the strengths of this process, but here's what I think is among its biggest; it's very difficult for employees to argue their raise. They can disagree with managers about their performance appraisal ratings, as people will; if the manager's doing his job, the company's reply to that employee is that the manager is acting within the legitimate scope of his judgment. But the actual increase is determined by an unarguable function of math, one reason managers and employees with whom I've worked who have used this process have reported solid levels of satisfaction with it.

My Nominations for the HR Canon

Reading business books is like prospecting. You can find some precious nuggets that can change your life, but getting them requires endless hours of sifting through a lot of dreck. There are certainly thoughtful books on human resources being written (Dave Ulrich is a name you should get to know); but here are five that, in my humble opinion, represent the mother lode of wisdom in their respective subjects that I think every HR person should read.

- *The Effective Executive* by Peter Drucker. A fast read that will screw the new manager's head on straight.
- *Hire With Your Head* by Lou Adler. Best book on hiring in existence. The chapter on Position Results Descriptions is worth the price of the whole book.
- *Discipline Without Punishment* by Dick Grote. There aren't many books you could say are truly definitive on any topic, but this one really is. It's simply the only book about discipline you need to read.
- *How to Win Friends and Influence People* by Dale Carnegie. Don't let the white hair and funny glasses fool you; that guy wrote what is still the best book on leadership ever. Re-read it every three years.
- *Good to Great* by Jim Collins. The business world is only beginning to work through the implications of Collins' truly groundbreaking research, and in particular HR has yet to think through the ramifications of his conclusions on leadership.

Interviewing & Recruiting

Of all the skills required of an HR leader, few are more critical to success in the role than having a superior ability to interview. I don't say that because of the importance of selecting the right people for your organization. I say that because interviewing teaches you the fine art of learning from and about people – how to phrase a question to yield a substantive answer, how to interpret verbal and physical responses, how to shut up and let a person to talk, and then how to synthesize your data into a prediction about a course of action. Of all the things you could concentrate on early in your HR career that would lead to promotion, among the most profitable would be to do boatloads of interviewing. Do them for positions at every level of the organization – it gives you an invaluable overview of your employee population and its needs.

*

Now, to help you become that superior interviewer, I'm going to give you an invaluable truth that you don't come across much, and you'll have to chew on for a while to really understand. Ready?

It takes no skill at all to identify a true superstar player in an interview. That person will make her capabilities known to the interviewer, and there won't be much anyone can do about it. Similarly, it takes no skill at all to identify the completely unsuited person in an interview. Even my junior high-aged son could determine that I'm not fit to be a biologist. If you accidentally get the right person, or a really good person, you win. The real skill in interviewing lies in being able to weed out the *almost* suitable candidate – the person who has a lot of what the company is looking for, but not everything. Those are the people who suck up all your company's time with coaching, disciplining, and firing. The real goal of your interviewing process should be to weed out the almost suitable.

*

Most experienced interviewers have their nearly sure-fire indicators of a good or bad hire. Here are mine, starting with what I call the Red Flags. If one of them is waving, it's probably time to politely wrap up the interview and send the candidate the heck out your door for good:

- No sense of humor. Honestly, if I can't get someone to laugh, I don't want to work with her.
- Boastfulness
- Leaders who don't acknowledge the efforts of the team
- Running down a current/former employer or supervisor
- Being late
- Odd explanations for major life decisions
- No responsibility for failures
- And the number one Red Flag: Inability to substantiate a declaration. A candidate for a leadership role told me her greatest leadership strength was her ability to develop staff. I replied, "That's great. So tell me about your biggest success story with developing a staff member." She responded by telling me about her firm belief in the

criticality of developing team members. I said, "I couldn't agree more. So tell me about the career of your most successful protégé?" Again, more about the view on staff development from 50,000 feet. I hope she's found a nice career, wherever she ended up.

Conversely, these are what I consider the Green Flags, which tell you it's probably time to think about putting together a competitive offer:
- Evidence of company recognition, such as big raises, promotions, or special assignment.
- Evidence of hard work
- Intelligence
- Humility
- A desire to make a contribution to the organization or one's profession

*

Oddly enough, the IT revolution and rise of the Internet have not made recruiting more a matter of technology; it has made recruiting much more a question of marketing. When candidates can compare your image and employer value proposition with your competitors in a matter of minutes, employer branding is not an esoteric issue you can afford to tackle "someday;" you need to buy your Marketing guy a few lunches and be certain you're presenting an image that will attract the right people.

*

A good recruiting process does more than encourage the right people to apply; it also discourages the wrong people from applying. The key is to provide people the right information up front so they can make the decision either that they have just for their dream company, or that you're not right for them. Think about that when you're evaluating your company's hiring portal.

*

When developing qualifications for an open position, everybody goes first to education, then years of experience. The lawyers love to see employers use those as criteria because they're very helpful for weeding out unqualified people who want to accuse us of discrimination. If I say I need someone with five years' experience, and you've got four, it's hard for you to claim I didn't hire you for reasons not related to the job.

But the reality is that just because somebody has done something a lot, does not mean they've done it well. So never, ever equate time on a job to adequate job knowledge or capability. Drill into that experience requirement with the hiring team as you're developing your search criteria; why do they say they need someone with seven years on this job? What desired knowledge or capabilities do they think that time frame represents? Not only does it give you a clearer picture of the job you're looking to fill; more importantly, it helps the rest of the hiring team develop a clearer consensus around what successful performance looks like.

*

When filling entry- or low-level positions, you may come across a candidate with a few jobs on his resume who is very well spoken; he's sociable, has good eye contact, a good sense of humor. In fact, you wonder if this person might be supervisory material, despite the fact that he's had no such experience.

You may also notice that his references contain co-workers only. In such situations, ask yourself whether you could see him as a natural used-car salesman. If you answer yourself with a yes, be very careful about him. Insist on getting references from supervisors, and if he can't produce them, you need to decide that he's not likely to be a good fit. Trust me, he's not.

That wasn't supervisory potential or strong social skills you were seeing; that was a creep who was trying to charm you. People with those kinds of interpersonal abilities who are also good hires put them to use for something productive; they really do sell things, or become leaders, and it shows up on their resumes. People who have those skills and have nothing to show for them in their careers are that way because they have no intention of doing so. They put those abilities to work trying to wriggle out of attendance problems or convince you and doctors that they've had "injuries." Leave those snakes in the grass where you found them.

*

If your company has a good receptionist, treat that person like gold and don't let her leave if you have to get down on bended knee with flowers and tears. I think everybody who works appreciates a good receptionist - and the HR department doesn't stop hearing about a bad one. Not only is a good receptionist important to your department's peace of mind; it's the worst job to recruit for. Every slovenly, disorganized misanthrope who can type will clog your server with their irrelevant resumes, imagining themselves to be the perfect gatekeeper for and face of your organization. Slogging through them to get to that one, precious person who really can pick up after your organization without being an annoying mother hen, *and* who can make a positive, professional first impression, is like the quest for the Holy Grail of applicants.

If there's any position for which you need a good prescreening process, it's for the receptionist. (Most Accounting positions are close runners-up.)

Dealing With the Problem Children

This is going to sound weird, but I have found it invariably to be true. When you start a new job as an HR leader, at some point in your first month or so there will be at least two people a notch or two below you on the org chart who will go out of their way to be really welcoming to you. They'll be all smiles and chattiness, listen to you with almost rapt attention, and make eye contact with you from 50 feet down the hallway.

Sorry to have to tell you this, but these people – to whom you're looking to validate your self-image as an "approachable" leader, and on whom you're counting to spread the word about what a great HR person you are – are going to be among your first problem children.

It's not just that they're trying to get on your good side before their checkered pasts catch up with them. Oh, that's true in a few cases; but usually it's a little more complicated. That eagerness to make a good impression on you is often borne of a frustration. These tend to be people who feel the business is not recognizing their abilities or their accomplishments, and their attention to you is a first step in you fixing that for them. Unfortunately for them, there are reasons why the business isn't showering them with the raises, promotions, or accolades of which they believe themselves deserving – and those are the reasons that will bring these people to your office.

At the other end of the spectrum, you can pick out many of the best of the performers when you're new on the job because their behavior is the exact opposite. These are people who hustle past you in the hallways with a quick nod and a distracted half-smile, who take months before they can so much as mumble your name. They're not avoiding you because they're afraid of coming under your attention; they just have more important things to think about than human resources. "HR person," they think when – if - they glance at you. "That's who I call when I have a benefits question." Then their thoughts immediately return to their more valuable train of delivering results. Don't let this ambivalence towards you hurt your feelings; just gratefully leave these people to the business of paying your salary.

Oh, but don't worry – they aren't likely to be the worst you'll encounter!

In the course of your career you'll likely work alongside some steely-sharp leaders; people who can slice through data to chart the future for the business, who will chop off negotiating partners at the knees and make it feel like it was a sweetheart kiss. Yet, when these people have an employee problem, they're going to show up outside your door for help. Early in my career a wise, experienced Ops guy once told me, "When you're a manager, 80% of everything you do could be done by most anybody who works for you. It's the other 20% where you really earn your money." Many of the problem children are part of your 20%.

Helping Managers Deal with their Problem Children

Training managers and supervisors in coaching and disciplining employees is one of the very best ways I know for a new HR leader to earn the respect of an organization's leadership team. In fact, doing it will do more than just earn their respect; in most cases you'll earn their gratitude. Most untrained managers aren't very good at stepping up to address disciplinary problems, and they know it. For some it really churns their guts at night. Give your managers a good training program in coaching and disciplinary techniques, supported by a formal disciplinary system, and you'll be giving them what they regard as some of the most valuable tools in their toolbox – not to mention a better night's sleep.

*

Let's get one thing straight about coaching employees with problems: The purpose of any coaching or disciplinary discussion is not "to make the person aware" she has a problem. It's not to get her to think about something differently; employees are not paid for specific cognitive processes. It's also not about just building up documentation to get ready to fire somebody (well, at least most of the time). The purpose of your discussion is to get this person to change her behavior. Notice I said "get *this person* to change:" *You* can't change anybody but yourself. If you could, chances are your spouse would be a very different person. (My spouse is the first to agree with me on this!)

Less thoughtful or skilled managers see their employee problems as "attitude problems." If you're going to help them deal appropriately with their problem children, changing that understanding of their problem is where you have to start. So when you do your coaching/discipline training, one of the first lessons you need to give them is that they can't manage attitudes; their job is to manage behavior. Now, delivering that message to some will generate, shall we say, pushback. So let them finish snorting about how little you know about The Real World outside your cushy HR ivory tower, and then give them arguments such as these to enlighten their benighted minds. "Attitude is not what matters most, and you don't really believe that it does. Do you only give raises to happy people? Suppose you go to your boss to ask for a raise for one of your people, and he says, "Are you kidding? That guy can't get anything done right, and he's always late for work." Suppose then you reply, "yeah but he's got a great attitude!" Does that make your argument? And do you really fight for raises for those kinds of employees?

"Think about this: Suppose you have a new employee. After he's been on the job about two weeks, you walk up to him and ask, 'so, how's it going?' He replies, 'Aw man, I have to tell you – it's going great. Joining this company was the best decision I ever made. In my last job, I had stretches where I hated just getting up in the morning. Now I'm actually glad to get up! My wife tells me she's seen a huge improvement in me since I started here. I couldn't be happier!'

"Now, that's a great attitude, isn't it? (Watch the heads bob in enthusiastic agreement.) How many of you would like to have this guy working for you? Watch every hand in the room shoot up.
(Nod slowly with an arch smile on your face) "Oh, really? Well, suppose you ask this guy, 'So, what is it you like so much about working here?' And he replies, 'Are you kidding? I've been late for work four times since I started, and nobody has said a word to me! My first week I smashed up a piece of equipment – must have cost $5000 – and I haven't heard boo about it! I smoke right under the No Smoking sign every day, and the President of the place walks right by and says good morning! What's not to like? I'm so glad I'm working (point to the audience for emphasis) for *you*!"
(Wait for the sheepish laughter to die down) "So *now* how many of you want this guy? (More sheepish chuckles and head shakes) What? Come on! I thought he was great! You loved the guy's attitude a second ago - what's wrong with him now?"

Once they answer and you summarize you may move on with your training, secure in the knowledge that your audience recognizes the truth of managing behavior and not attitude.

Coaching Techniques

As Dick Grote writes in *Discipline Without Punishment* (have
you ordered it yet?), coaching is about gaining an employee's
agreement to behave a certain way. One technique he suggests
for getting that agreement is to point out the consequences of
behaving appropriately and of behaving inappropriately: "You
can choose to continue coming to work late, and eventually
lose your job, or you can come to work on time and remain
employed and a valued member of the team; which will it be?"
Here are two other techniques that I find to be very effective:

We've scratched your back; how about you scratch ours?
Simple reciprocity is pretty hard to argue with. Leverage any
benefits the person has received in the employment
relationship, like, "Your supervisor did some of your work so
you could attend the optional personal finance training, and she
gave you a really decent raise last time around. So she's made
a personal effort to help you out, and she's recognized the solid
work you've done last year. So she's working with you; how
about you start working with her and do the job the way we
need it done?"

Sounds a lot like putting a guilt trip on a person? Whatever.
There's a reason why your overbearing mother-in-law does that
to you. Any time you can cast your request for agreement as a
return for consideration the company has shown to an
employee, you're placing yourself in a very powerful position.

It's a simple fix. This is one I got from Dale Carnegie's book (have you ordered that one yet?). Point out that you're not asking for perfection, or for an impossibly high standard; you just need the person to do what's required. "Look, I know it's hard to get to work on time sometimes, but we all have to do it. I have to get in on time, your co-workers have to get in on time – heck, the VP of Operations has to get in on time. We're not asking for the moon here; we just need you to meet the same expectation that all of us have to meet. So what do you say?"

*

When you're addressing an employee about a problem that has repeated itself, it's infinitely better to be too blunt than too sparing of the person's feelings. Ooh, that sounds mean, doesn't it? Well, don't forget – you're talking about a person's career. He's a got a mortgage, a family, hopes for the future. Which do you think he'd prefer a bruised ego or the unemployment line? Which do you think his family would prefer?

I said earlier that you can't change anybody; but at the same time, your job is to help the person recognize that different choices have different consequences, and sometimes you have to deliver that help right between the eyes.
Of course you don't need to yell or beat him about the head; but if there's a better than even chance that a person's behavior is jeopardizing his job, that's a punch you owe him not to pull.

*

The only fair way to deal with most employee problems is to put the person on notice that there is a problem, be clear about what it is, and give her a reasonable opportunity to correct it. Does it really work? Sometimes, usually for the more routine issues like conduct problems. Every now and then people really do turn serious problems around, just frequently enough to convince you that addressing the next one may not be a complete waste of everybody's time. But most people's capacities for hard work or integrity are pretty well in place by the time they join your organization, and there's generally little you can do to change them; and unless you're working for a social welfare organization, well, you have to remember that you're not a social welfare organization.

When confronting the overwhelming majority of problem children, you shouldn't start off with the goal of firing the person; but at times that will end up being your goal. In some extreme cases, reaching your goal will require an exorbitant expenditure of your company's time, until you'll think your department's entire role has been redefined to deal with this one miscreant.

That can get pretty frustrating if you let it; and I'll bet that one day that person's manager will show up in your office, gravely presenting to you some new piece of information about the problem child. "Look at these records of his Internet activity during work hours," she'll say with a furrowed brow and steady voice, as though she's discovered her boy is leading an international smuggling ring. "He's doing an awful lot of personal surfing during work time. I can't have this in my department, and besides, this is against company policy! Now we can fire him!"

Then you pick through her data, and establish a) he probably has some web pages up for long periods because he's toggling between personal web activity and work; b) neither of you can say with any confidence at this point that this activity is really any more excessive than anybody else's – and it probably isn't; and let's not forget c) the IT people really shouldn't have let this manager go fishing around an employee's computer usage without authorization. Sorry, you tell the manager, you're really not ready to pull the trigger. On hearing your verdict her shoulders droop, she sighs, shakes her exasperated head, and pleads, "Can't we just *fire this guy?"*

This is when you need to draw strength from the example of one of HR's patron saints, the TV detective Columbo (man, am I showing my age?). Columbo matched wits with some pretty clever and obnoxious criminals, who were always careful to have an alibi or otherwise cover their tracks while practically daring him to arrest them for the crime. But Columbo never got riled, never lost his head and arrested somebody before he knew he could make it stick. He just kept plodding along, patiently keeping his eyes and ears open while he gathered and reviewed his evidence, until bam! Somewhere, somehow, the criminal screwed up. And when he did, our hero was right there in his rumpled raincoat to haul another reprobate off to the pokey.

Remind your frustrated manager that nobody gets away with it forever. Really. (Unless you're in a union house, where people really do get away with it forever.) You can't make so important a decision based on frustration. We're paid to make prudent decisions for our employer; we don't have the luxury of making them to satisfy our emotions.

Sooner or later your problem child will screw up again. They all do. And when he does, if you're gathering your facts and documenting them, you'll be there to hold the person accountable once and for all. There's no need for a dirty bust.

*

Many of your handbook's policies end with the line, "violation of this policy is subject to disciplinary action, up to and including termination of employment." For most of your employee problems the decision of whether to discipline or to terminate someone will be fairly clear. But every so often somebody will hand you some weird, one-off problem that is serious enough to give you reason to consider terminating the person, and for which neither your handbook nor precedent offer much to guide your decision making. How do you figure out when to give the person a note to the file or a boot out the door?

Of course, you should start by considering the precedent you'll be setting. But I think it's a mistake to make your decision based on a future set of circumstances that are impossible to foresee, and for a problem that isn't likely to reoccur anyway. Besides, precedent is only one of several factors to weigh in such a decision. Don't forget an individual's work record. We need to hold people accountable for their actions, but only so much for the judgment of posterity.

In these situations I think this is the key question: Does he get it? if you discipline the person, what is your estimate of the likelihood that you'll be back here again? Does the person understand the impact of his actions, and does he express sincere regret for it? If he does, he's given you a reason to invest your credibility in going to bat for him to the rest of management. But if instead he points fingers, talks about why it's not his fault, he's not giving you much reason to turn him loose on the employee population again. In that case, you've got reason to let him loose from the business.

*

Here's a little technique that I find helpful when going into a disciplinary discussion with a problem child that I believe will get contentious. (No, I don't think the HR leader should conduct all the disciplinary discussions; but I do think it's helpful when it's a potentially difficult discussion and the person's manager isn't experienced enough.)

When we have discussions with people, including disciplinary meetings, it's often from behind a desk. We might believe that being able to see a person's full body when they can't see ours would give us something of an edge, but it can often appear that we're hiding behind a barrier. For all the other person knows, your knees are knocking. So if you think it's going to get a little testy, arrange the seating so there is nothing but space between you and the employee. If your office is arranged so that you'd have to talk to the employee across your desk, sit on a chair next to the employee. If you have to use a conference room, sit on the same side of the table, not on the other side.

The problem child may try to intimidate you, but that will be much harder when - and this is the key to making this work – she sees that you are perfectly relaxed. Cross a leg with an ankle over the knee, cup the back of your neck with your hand for a bit, or stretch. Above all, keep your body very loose. Demonstrating that you're comfortable with the tension will also communicate that you're comfortable with your position – and then your problem child will wish she had a desk to hide behind.

*

This is a close as I've ever come to a works-every-time response to a particular employee problem. Every so often an otherwise good employee will lose his or her cool, and go on a swearing and ranting rampage about the building. Those disruptive episodes belong in the category of Cannot Under Any Circumstances Be Tolerated in the Workplace. So before the Tasmanian Devil has spun himself out, send him home for an emergency suspension. Tell him you'll call him when you've decided what to do; and then for the next few days, don't. Let him sweat as he stares into the abyss of unemployment. Don't call until after he has called the company, wondering what's to become of him. In that conversation, tell him you haven't finished your investigation. When you finally do call him back, he will be one whipped pup. Is that manipulative of me? Unenlightened of me? Guilty as charged. But every would-be Unholy Terror who was shown that abyss stepped back – for good.

*

Many people believe managers should conduct disciplinary discussions exclusively. I think HR should be involved in later stages of progressive discipline, and whenever practicable, should be involved in terminations, especially for reasons of willful misconduct. For one thing, managers won't do this enough to get "good" at it, and no amount of training will prepare the newer manager for the emotions that often come into play (for the lucky few who do get good at it, though, let them at it).

Also, having HR on hand demonstrates that the decision has been reviewed by a third party, and is the decision of the company; thus, it's harder for the ex-employee to convince himself he was unfairly treated. But most importantly, when the issue is one of willful misconduct, HR can more effectively represent the company at the inevitable unemployment compensation appeals hearing.

*

Conducting Investigations

I'm putting this under the heading of Doing Investigations, but it also belongs under a discussion of Interviewing, or under Everything You Will Ever Do in Human Resources. The less experienced at making decisions in HR often believe that making people decisions like hiring, or weighing evidence in an investigation, is often a matter of intuition – of "going with your gut." Those folks would do well to remember the advice a chess grandmaster once gave for those who wanted to play the game well. He said you should always play as though someone is standing over your shoulder who can read your mind.

Every time you seriously consider a move, that guy is pointing to the piece and asking, "why would you do that?" If you can't give that guy a cogent explanation, it's a bad move. It may objectively be the right move; but if you don't understand its implications, you won't be prepared for handling what comes later. The right move, poorly understood, will prove a mistake in the long run.

That guy is out there in every HR person's life (really, in every manager's life). He goes by many names – The Boss, General Opinion, Your Honor, Ladies and Gentlemen of the Jury; and not having an answer for him when he's asking why you hired or fired someone can cost you a lot more than your king. So forget about your gut; pay attention to that guy over your shoulder.

91

Now, before I go on, I need to interject something: I like to believe I start from thinking the best about people until proven otherwise, but what you're about to read is going to sound pretty cynical. I can only say I write this because, like everything else in this book, my experience has shown me it is true.

One of the problems with gut decisions is that they're based on your *impressions* of what's true, and when you're conducting an employee investigation, a lot of people will do anything to give you an impression of what's true – even when it's not. I have known several people whose behavior came under my scrutiny in an investigation, people whose integrity I had hitherto never had cause to question. In many of these situations, they showed a remarkable facility with faking sincerity and lying. One guy implored me to look in his eyes, and ask if I really thought he could lie to me while looking straight at me. It turned out that, as a matter of fact, he could. And he's been far from the only one.

The fear of losing a job brings out the worst in many people. Maybe they wouldn't *do* "anything" to avoid that consequence for their actions, but many people have no problem with *saying* anything to avoid it. (By the way, don't think I'm sneering down from on high here; I recognize full well that a) I've never been in that situation, and b) I've got a wife and kids of my own to feed.)

We all want to believe the best about people, including co-workers, but here's a hard truth: People can lie. And when their jobs are on the line, people can lie well.

Just about everybody flatters himself or herself on being a good judge of character. Just about everybody thinks his or her gut could help them see through somebody's lies in a pinch. Just about everybody is wrong.

I can promise you that you will have a few investigations into employee problems in which the facts point to an employee's guilt, but his protestations of innocence are so sincere you'll hear violins, and they will cause you to doubt your conclusion. If your conclusion is based on facts, don't. More than once, as a miscreant artiste turned ex-employee was being accompanied out of the building following his termination, he was asked by the escorting supervisor, "you did it, didn't you?" and the answer was, "yeah, I did."

The great thing about facts is that they add up. Facts will satisfy that guy standing over your shoulder. Facts make sense. So the next time you're conflicted between your gut feel and the facts, tell your gut thanks for the input, and go with the facts.

*

The most challenging point in any employee investigation for an HR person is not when you're weighing the facts; your sexual harassment or even your theft problems will not demand the sleuthing prowess of CSI: Milwaukee or whatever. No, I

93

think the hardest part for us to get right is the very first meeting, just after that phone call when an employee has asked with hesitation in her voice, "can I talk to you about something?"

What could be so difficult about that, you ask? Let me explain it this way:

You might be familiar with medieval romances about King Arthur and the Knights of the Round Table. Many of them have a similar story line: One day Sir Galahad is out riding his horse in full battle armor (don't ask why - it's a knight thing) when he sees a beautiful young maiden by the road, weeping. He asks what the matter is, and through heartfelt sobs she tells him of the evil black knight who has imprisoned her true love in yon tower. Sir Galahad is incensed at the injustice, and overcome with pity for the young creature; and before you can say forsooth and anon, valiant Galahad has bashed in the tower door, killed the black knight, and freed the girl's sweetheart, to leave the young couple swooning in gratitude.

Now, maybe that passed for sound jurisprudence in the twelfth century, but if you or I tried that we'd likely find one little complication: As the black knight gasps for his last breath, he tells us that the guy he'd imprisoned had stolen five of his best cattle. Hmm – funny, we'd think with sword drooping in hand as the black knight crumples to the ground in an iron heap; she'd kinda left that part out.

Of course, this little story illustrates the dangers of acting before we have all the facts; but you didn't need me to tell you that. Here's the bigger question: what caused our good Galahad to dash off and kill somebody who didn't deserve to die? The problem is not because he's evil; the problem is, he's trying to be good - or we should say, he's trying to be a certain kind of good. Not the kind that gives alms to the poor, or takes care of wayward children.

Galahad is trying to be a hero. However, not every situation that requires a good outcome demands a hero, someone who takes big, bold, splashy steps to accomplish something that people can admire. You might say the problem is that Galahad is trying to fulfill a persona. And unfortunately for Galahad (and the black knight), he found someone who wanted him to fulfill that persona.

Remember what I'd said earlier about the HR persona, the expectations people have about the kind of person people think you should be? I said that, while you can't be considered successful if you don't live up to it, there is a danger of taking it too far. Well, you will likely run that danger almost every time an employee presents you with a problem he or she is having with another employee. And you have to recognize that the danger has two dimensions. One is that the employee wants you to be more than the HR person; she wants you to be her knight in shining armor – Righter of Wrongs, Defender of the Weak and Infirm. The other is that, let's face it – to a certain extent, that's who you'd like to be.

Look, you went into human resources, not administrative justice. Yes, you want to be a business partner, and well you should. But somewhere inside, you went into this job because you do want to do good for people when you can. And when someone tells you about what sounds like sexual harassment, or discrimination, or just plain nastiness, you want to help. In fact, you're in a position to help.

But ask yourself this, and be honest: When this person comes to you with her tale of woe, injustice, or peril, why, in your role as HR leader, do you want to do good? Is it truly because you want to help her? Or like the knights in tales of yore, is it because you want to win renown? Or maybe you want to use this situation to confirm your self-image as a really good person? If a yes is twitching somewhere in the back of your brain, congratulations on your honesty. Remember that next time someone is in your office describing a problem with a co-worker or supervisor.

It's not that your indulgence in the rush of Righteous Indignation is going to cause you to dash out and fire the accused black knight. You're not that dumb. You will talk to that other employee and maybe other witnesses, and you'll get to the right conclusion. But as you do, you'll discover that there were some pretty important facts that that person had not given you, facts that make it clear that the accused person did not deserve your righteous indignation after all. If you had described the problem to your boss or a relevant peer after having spoken only to the complaining employee, you might have let slip an expression or two of disapproval of the accused employee that was undeserved, and now you have to backtrack it. And if you had been overtly sympathetic to the employee, giving her the impression that you were on her side, you'll have to tell her that you're not giving her what she wants after all. Most people find that pretty jarring and it can leave some hard feelings that just didn't have to be left (not that it should; it just does). Do you get to the right place in the end? Sure, and good for you. But there were some unnecessarily ragged edges to the outcome that would keep me from giving you the A for professionalism.

By the way, do people deliberately omit certain facts when they accuse another employee of some malfeasance? Sometimes, but not usually. Do people try to manipulate you? You betcha. But I think in most cases, it's just that people tell you the facts they believe are relevant. Our damsel in distress loves the thief; what caused the black knight to take her love from her isn't important to her. That's why it's really hard to get all the facts from one person.

If you sincerely want to do good things for people at times like this, then save your inner Sir Galahad for world hunger and just do your job. When dealing with employee disputes, be fair-minded, patient, and respectful of employees involved in disputes. Investigate thoroughly, weigh the facts, and act on your conclusions. Doing all that will take more of your time than you'll prefer to spend on these issues, and you'll seldom leave the parties involved weeping for joy by the roadside as you trot off on your trusty steed. But more than having done good, you'll have done your job.

*

Of course, there are times when you can count among your problem children those who are paid to be the grown-ups – your supervisors, managers, directors, and vice presidents. That group is capable as any other of malfeasance, and you have to be ready for anything. However, I'd like to offer you this perspective on what to prepare for. Our society invests enormous wealth in eliminating various forms of discrimination. How badly is it needed, really?

In all my years, I have never encountered a bona fide instance in which a manager or supervisor wanted to make an employment decision based on someone's race. In fact, the sum total of my experience with race in the workplace is a single employee using a single racial epithet. I have never encountered discrimination on the basis of one's sexual orientation, to the extent that that is prohibited in certain locales. I have encountered only one instance of gender discrimination, and it was not committed by some relic of another era. I have certainly never encountered a disparaging remark or action directed towards veterans. I think it's because of two forces at work. For one, mores around these things really have changed. For another, the war for talent is too real to allow any organization the luxury of indulging in personal biases.

But don't cue the singing birds just yet. There is one form of discrimination that many managers will commit without the slightest compunction. Confronting it will require you to challenge opinions that are sincerely held as necessary for the business. When managers talk about the need to bring in "fresh" talent, they generally mean "young" talent. "Under 40" talent. Age discrimination is for real, and in all too many cases, managers really don't care whether they commit it or not. You will have times in which you need to remind your peers, and your boss, that it is against your company's EEO policy and against the law.

HR Metrics

For all that's been written over the years about human resources metrics, it seems our profession has yet to settle on a definitive set of measures to the extent that, say, the Accounting or Operations worlds have. So it's worth your time to experiment to see what makes sense in your organization. But never forget that the most important metrics to HR are those that the rest of your organization uses to measure quality, productivity, and profitability. Above all others, those are the numbers you're there to move. So as you are experimenting with metrics to track, if you can't show how a metric ties to those used by the rest of the business, keep it off your dashboard.

*

Believe it or not, one of the most difficult questions to answer is, "how many people do we have in this organization?" The problem with counting the heads at a given moment is that the number of heads will likely change in the next moment, as positions open and fill, are created and then eliminated . And if headcount is the subject of a management meeting, and the only prep notes you're given is to "just give us the number," chances are somebody's going to start picking apart that number. "Why is it six people higher than last month?" "Did we have people quit? Who?" And so on. In these situations, try to keep the "ummm…"s to a minimum while you rack your brains for answers.

If this describes your management team, start tracking the approved positions. In some ways, the number of positions approved is a more realistic picture of headcount than actual headcount, because it reflects what management says it needs to run the operation.

*

Besides the ones you find in the books and web articles, here are two metrics I find really worthwhile:

- Hires vs. Voluntary Terminations by Month. We track this as a cumulative line graph, with hires shown as a solid line and terminations a dotted line. The current and two prior years are color coded. This chart has more than once alerted us to challenges on both the recruiting and the retention sides.

- Hiring Source Effectiveness. We ask all incoming employees to tell us which was the one recruiting source that convinced them to send us their resume. Sort that by year, and see how the effectiveness of different sources changes over time. For us, that has uncovered overspends with third-party recruiters, and problems with a recruiting technology change we once made.

As these offerings suggest, the HR metrics field is trying to move toward real predictive analytics. I think that the work being done these days on data analysis is perhaps the most important in the HR field. If you aren't familiar with the thinking and emerging practices related to HR analytics, get familiar.

What I've Learned About Leadership

You can't take ten steps in business without tripping over somebody's advice on leadership. Well, please look down before you take another step, because here come a few observations of mine on the subject:

*

I'm trying to keep this kind of thing to the barest of minimums, but I'm going to repeat two observations made by others only because I keep bumping up against these over and over in my career. After my share of travel on several continents, reading of world history, and cracking 50 (after the references to "Star Trek" and "Colombo," I'm sure you're shocked), I've concluded that, beyond the biological functions, there are only two traits that are truly universal to all human beings: a longing for transcendence, and a sense of failure to live up to one's own expectations (there - that's as deep as I get). But somewhere in the next rank of True For Most People But Not Really Everybody If You Stop And Think About It, are these:

One: Most people want to win. They want to play on a winning team.

Two: Most of the time, people conform to expectations. That is commonly understood as meaning if you set goals for people, most people most of the time will work to achieve them. But it also means as a leader, you have to be clear about in your own mind about your expectations for your people -

because for better or worse they're what you'll get. Do you believe people can't be trusted to do their own work? If so, you'll run a department of automatons who won't think for themselves.

*

Never BS people. Ever. I promise you, you will be found out. Early in my career I formulated this little maxim: You're never as smart as you think you are, and they're never as dumb as you sometimes wish they were.

*

There are two common ways to ruin your credibility as a leader. The first is to BS people. The second is to make a commitment and then fail to follow through on it. It is possible to overcome the first, in time. It is virtually impossible to overcome the second. Ever. That failure will stick in people's guts and it will not come out. You want to tell yourself that people's memory of your failure will fade over time. It will not. So even if a certain commitment is the right thing to do, if you don't plan on following it through, for God's sake don't make it.

*

One of the most powerful rewards for good people is your trust. Let these people know they have that (once they've earned it), and they will walk through walls to keep it.

*

Be slightly, *slightly* paranoid. Spend a little time each week with that little guy looking over your shoulder in the chess story a few pages back. A mortal dread of spectacular failure is a great motivator to cover all your bases (at least it's worked for me). And in these days of hair-trigger litigation you need him to help keep your organization – and you personally - from getting sued.

*

I found this excellent line in General George Patton's memoir, and I'm surprised I've never seen it quoted elsewhere: "A good plan executed now is better than a perfect plan executed later." Early in my career, when I was both supremely confident in my abilities and supremely ignorant of how hard it is to get big things done, I used to search for The Big Solution to business challenges. I was convinced that every solution had to be the big, ultimate kind, perfectly conceived to anticipate all contingencies. And therefore, it took me a long time to get anything done – if I got anything done at all.

Organizations are hives of other people's goals that have nothing in common with yours. Getting enough of those people to incorporate your goals into their own is immensely difficult (how willing are you to incorporate their goals into yours, after all?). Getting something done is usually better than getting nothing done (except in the case of performance appraisals done badly). Getting something done well usually comes after getting practice just doing something. I'm not excusing mediocrity; I'm warning you against allowing your relentless pursuit of perfection to become the eternal search for a firm completion date.

When you're starting something ambitious and new to you, there's a point at which continuing to anticipate the contingencies has a lower net value to the organization than just getting on with it and refining it as you go. Yes, you risk ruining the credibility of your entire initiative, but, then again, if it's new to you, you risk that anyway.

Just as, as I said earlier, every system can be gamed, so too does every solution have strengths and drawbacks. The trick – whether it's performance appraisals, or compensation plans, or most everything in life – is to select one whose strengths gets you closest to your goals, and whose drawbacks can most effectively be minimized. Offering solutions is like tossing out shark bait – there are sharp-toothed animals out there dying to rip them to shreds. But you can't be a leader if you're afraid of those waters.

*

This is some of the best advice I ever heard for a leader: Read. Read a lot, and don't ever stop. It doesn't matter what – just read. Inspiration is most always the result of a synthesis of knowledge, and you can't synthesize knowledge if you don't have any. The best way to get it is to read.

*

This little observation is offered with a spoonful of cynicism to help it go down. For all the gallons of ink spilled (or in the Digital Age, maybe we should say terabytes of black pixels generated) about how leaders must inspire and motivate their people, I find it remarkable how so many of the most effective leaders I've worked with don't do much of either in any conscious way.

They'd be the first to tell you that they're pretty boring when addressing a group; having a narrow range of emotions themselves, they're not much good at tapping into those of others. Yet their people give these leaders their best. How can that be?

They are good leaders because they're just good at what they do. They get done what they say they're going to get done. They don't ask anybody to do anything they won't do themselves; in fact, they work harder than everybody else. Above all, they know their stuff. Good people are attracted to those characteristics, and before you know it, there's that winning team on which most people want to play.
Napoleon Bonaparte was a gifted solider of astonishing charisma; yet without question, the source of that charisma was the fact that he was just really, really good at what he did, and everybody knew it. However, the man who beat Napoleon at Waterloo, the Duke of Wellington, never inspired the fanatical devotion in his men of which Napoleon was capable. Napoleon's men affectionately called him their "little corporal;" Wellington's men called him Nosey, for reasons you

can guess. Napoleon spoke affectionately to his men, often calling them his "children;" Wellington called his army at Waterloo "scum." He was distant even with most of his senior staff.

Not much evidence of motivational techniques there, so why did the British stand for Wellington through the horrors of Waterloo? Because Wellington won battles – a lot. He had mastered the details of his field thoroughly. He was everywhere and anywhere he needed to be, for as long as it took, to get the job done. He didn't go in much for the ego-boosting, inspirational aspects of leadership; he just put his oversized nose to the grindstone and kept it there. The result was a remarkable string of victories, often against long odds, and an unarguable demonstration of ability that in itself brought out the best in his subordinates. That's what held together his little armies through hardship to victory after victory.

I'm not holding up Wellington's leadership capabilities as inherently superior to Napoleon's - Napoleon was still a far better Emperor than Wellington ever was a later Prime Minister (and an even bigger workaholic). I'm just trying to illustrate that solid technical ability in a field can be just as valid a source of effective leadership ability as a reliance on other leadership abilities that fill the titles of leadership books today.

That's hardly an original observation; in fact there's even a term for it. The Big Thinkers call Wellington's style relying on his "referent" power. So many modern leadership gurus chastise companies for promoting their technical experts to leadership roles, heedless of their interpersonal leadership skills (as the gurus define them). For example, the best tool and die maker is often made the shift supervisor. That should be valid on its face, but the fact that so many organization do it is evidence of the fact that, much more often than not, it works. Above all, the person in charge has to know how things work around here.

Why is this reality seldom acknowledged in the leadership literature? Here's where that cynicism trickles in. I think the real reason is that leadership gurus can quote Napoleons and Wellingtons (and Sun Tzus and Lee Iaccocas and…); they can do research on their own and synthesize it with that of others to write interesting books that today's business reading public would buy. But they can't write a saleable book telling generals how to better fight battles AND telling purchasing people how to purchase things better AND telling HR people how better to do human resources. Nobody's that smart. And assuming anybody could write it, how many people would buy it?

It's more saleable to focus on what people believe to be common to leadership in every situation. Which would you pay to tackle on a red-eye home; a collection of soaring anecdotes that celebrate the human spirit's ever-new desire to inspire those around them to success, or a tome on how to interpret federal and state regulatory guidance? Which would you rather write?

You're not going to find many leadership gurus willing to sell you training on the boring, tedious, technical aspects of particular fields as the stuff of leadership development. But just because those topics don't fill up airport bookshelves, don't think that someone can't parley such strengths and general work habits to become a successful leader.

Communication

"Strong communication skills." The phrase appears on almost every job's list of qualifications - including yours – and well it should. It also appears on almost every job seeker's resume – and well it shouldn't.

Let's be clear about one thing: The ability to reach into the grab bag of tired, hackneyed phrases used in most business writing and paste them together well enough to pass your word processing software's grammar checker does not qualify as "strong writing skills." I'm not saying that it takes a Thomas Paine to announce your next annual enrollment meetings (although, for HR, those often are the times that try men's souls!); but I am saying that, if your written communications are going to do what you need them to do, you do need to overcome two significant challenges.

I've just alluded to the first. Since the late 1980s the business world has been relying on the same limited vocabulary to inspire their workers and excite their customers. But after thirty-some years, like old workhorses that have served too many seasons, these words have become so worn out through overuse and misuse that they just aren't capable of doing the work they used to do. Here's just a partial list of words that deserve to spend most of your career put to pasture:

- Committed
- Driven
- Vision

- Excellence
- Passion

Learning organization (it still amazes me how few people have no idea what this term means. It was coined by Peter Senge in his book, "The Fifth Discipline," and contrary to what many people think, it doesn't mean a business that does a lot of training.)

Let me guess: Your organization is driven by its vision of excellence. Or maybe you're committed to your vision to be driven with passion. Or maybe you have a vision of commitment to excellence. No wait, I'm sure you're different – you have a passion for the PURSUIT of excellence! Relentlessly! I hear your yawn from here.

Now, a limited vocabulary might not be so bad were it not for the fact that we are living in the Hyper-Communication Age. I once read somewhere that the average American of today receives as much information in one month as an average 18th-century Frenchman would have consumed in his entire lifetime. We are bombarded and strafed with messages day after day, morning to night. So if you're really going to be an effective communicator on the job, you have to recognize that your challenge is to deliver messages that win the heavy competition for your employees' attention and get them to do what you need them to do. Just like your Marketing department, you have to cut through the chatter.

There's so much we could say about this, but here's the most important rule of effective communication: Don't be boring. Write stuff that people want to read. Say things in ways that people will want to listen to you.

Let's assume - *purely* for the sake of argument - that your organization's managers wait until the last minute to get their performance appraisals completed, if they're done on time at all. What do you do about it? Every few days you send out an e-mail reminder. Now, let me guess: These e-mails all have as the subject, "Performance appraisals." And every one of them reads: "Please remember that your performance appraisals are due to the HR department by Friday the 17th. Thanks." Why do you write these e-mails that way? Because you're very busy, you reply, and you don't have time to keep riding herd over these slow-moving cows.

Let me make another guess - your e-mails aren't working. Well, here's why: Because those cows are too busy even to open your same cow-like e-mail message over and over, let alone actually read it. (And by the way - if you start your e-mail with that hideous passive phrase "Please be reminded that…" you deserve to be ignored from spite!)

The next time you're about to write that e-mail, try this: Instead of writing "Performance appraisals," type "YOU'VE JUST WON THE NIGERIAN LOTTERY!" I'm not kidding. Then say this in your e-mail. "Well, not really. But now that I have your attention, please get your performance appraisals in to HR by Friday the 17th." When it gets down to the wire and Marvin in Accounting doesn't have his turned in for the umpteenth year in a row, send an e-mail with the subject line, "If you see Marvin in Accounting..." When everyone clicks to read the birthday wish, let them read, "Tell him to get his performance appraisals in to HR by Friday the 17th!" Trust me: You will have cured Marvin's tardiness.

Some time ago, my employer was offering an after-hours writing class to all employees. The last time the course had been offered, the attendance had been only so-so; but this time around we really wanted a good turnout. Now, I could have done the standard memo to all employees and probably be ignored about as much as had been the last announcement. But in my e-mail, I put a deliberate grammar mistake, and at my e-mail's conclusion, I said I would offer a small prize to the first two people who spotted the grammar error in this e-mail. My inbox was deluged with responses - and the class filled to overflow.

Of course my specific examples won't suit every communicator, or every organization's culture; you have to find your own voice. It doesn't have to be a voice that quickens every pulse, or even that parses every sentence. It just has to be interesting.

*

Usually, the written word is for relatively routine communications. When it's the harder news, like a sale of the business, or a RIF, or a decision to outsource a product line, it's usually more appropriate to do those in meetings. When you're delivering hard news, you have to do it in a way that shows you have an emotional investment in the outcome. I don't mean getting all weepy in front of people, or launching into some extended confession; these times are not about you and your feelings. But people have to see that it matters to you, and that their interests are your interests as well.

Your other challenge at these times is to show people how they should think and feel about this news. Call it propagandizing if you like; you're probably not working for a democracy of independent citizens. You have to get people through these times in ways that maintain their confidence in the organization, and that means you have to demonstrate that you appreciate the share the concerns of the rest of the employees, but that you recognize how this was a necessary step that can lead to better days ahead.

*

And if certain employees decide to use those meetings to put you on the spot with tough or even confrontational questions, don't stand where you are. Even if you're struggling for an answer, walk over to stand closer to the person asking the question (or making the speech, as the case may be). It shows you're not afraid of the question, or even the hostility of the questioner.

Workers Compensation

I hate workers compensation and everything to do with it. If you're part of a multi-state operation workers comp can get complicated. It can also be time consuming, frustrating, and above all, boring. However, it's one of the areas in which HR can deliver clearly identifiable savings to the bottom line, so you need to devote to the topic whatever time it requires.

*

The key to managing workers compensation claims is to manage them. Never, ever, ever let open claims sit for more than three hours. If there is a next step to be taken – follow up with a doctor, a supervisor's confirmation that a modified duty position will work for him – be sure you're taking it. These kinds of action items can fall into the "little things" category in the course of your department's activities and be allowed to slide, but these little things can add up to a lot of money.

*

To our continual annoyance, one of the things that seems perpetually to be on your insurance carrier's list of "little things" is the number of claims they list as open that should be closed. Don't assume that your carrier will know when that claimant has returned to work with no restrictions, or that, if the carrier does know, that they will actually close the claim as soon as they could. Call them and tell them to close that claim today. The best way to "encourage" prompt service from your claims manager is to be a perpetual pain in his rear.

*

Speaking of carriers; yours isn't going to tell you this, but you can argue reserves! Carriers will listen to you, and if you can present a solid case for lowering a reserve for a particular claim, they will do it. It doesn't always work – well, it doesn't usually work, but if you've got the facts for a claim with six-figure reserves, it's worth taking a run at it.

*

Don't leave any but the routine petitions to the carrier. If you have a petition before the workers compensation system, never assume that the attorney your carrier assigns you has the slightest idea about the facts in your case. No matter how fat the file, meet with the attorney before you have to appear before the referee or judge and make sure he understands what's been going on. If the hearing is going to involve testimony from a claimant who is less than trustworthy, you should attend. Sit at the table with the attorney and pass him a note if the claimant is less than honest in her testimony (shocking, I know, but it does happen). You should also read over medical depositions and don't be afraid to comment on them if the doc recounts information from the claimant that you know to be wrong.

*

Of course, we need to say a few words about those amoral slimeballs kindly referred to as "malingerers." There are those people who are so bound and determined to get time off at your company's expense that they will exaggerate any symptom, describe your workplace to their doctor as a chamber of horrors, and display an Orwellian capacity for rewriting simple truth. In the course of managing their claims (and that's usually a long, labor-intensive course), your boss may ask you, "don't you think we should just settle this claim and move on?" It's tempting to get this guy out of your life so you can get back to that thing called The Rest of Your Job. But If you've got the facts on your side, and cards left to play, your answer must be "no."

This is going to sound a little dark, but you have to *beat* these people. Your department and your boss are by no means the only ones who know what a treacherous swine this person is. Everybody else in the building knows it, too – and they're watching to see whether this person can get away with it. Some people are watching with no more interest than they'd bring to a tennis match. Most employees are likely on your company's side, because they know this person is swill and they don't like people who cheat. But there are several others who are quietly weighing their own chances of winning a fabulous cash prize courtesy of your workers compensation plan and whether they take their chances may well depend on the outcome of this current duel.

The best way you can persuade those people to stay honest and on the job is to win. It makes much more sense to go to the wall when you know you have a strong hand, even if that going is long, than to cut your losses this time only to face another challenger when you don't know what cards you'll be playing. You need to send that message that, if an employee is looking for some time off, he or she is not going to get it by faking an injury.

More than anything, these claims come down to contests of wills. Either you give up and settle, or they give up and come back to work or quit. These claims take doggedness, watchfulness, and above all patience (remember Columbo!), but they are battles worth fighting. When you're feeling frustrated about the expense of time and money, remember that your opponent's lying ways are costing him a lot more stress than they're costing you. After all, all the while his possible settlement is in question, you know you're still getting paid. And when you or your staff sit through the endless WC hearings – and you must, because your lawyer needs your input every step of the way – you can take comfort in the fact that the people at your table are the only ones being paid to be there, and will still be the only ones being paid all the while the clock is dragging on.

And as that clock drags on, that attorney's partners are likely pressuring her to get this case closed with even more urgency than your boss is to you. This kind of stress tends to work on these people over time, making them goofier and goofier until they say or do something that causes that workers comp judge and that doc finally to say "enough."

In workers comp as in war, there is no substitute for victory. But in your battles, follow Columbo's example - and take solace in the knowledge that you're fighting the good fight.

*

Finally, whatever distaste – or disgust – you may harbor for that particular breed of miscreants, don't let it color your view of every other claimant, or your company's other managers' view of those claimants. Remind yourself and them that the overwhelming majority of employees who get injured want nothing more than to get better and get back to work.

A Little Career Advice

These few thoughts could apply to just about anyone, but I include them because they're worth remembering even for an HR leader.

*

It's possible to be too successful in salary negotiations. When you get a company to pay someone more than they really wanted to pay for a job, you had better be worth it, because I guarantee you that, for the rest of your career, every time the boss looks at you, he'll be seeing that painfully large salary stamped right across your forehead - and you will get whacked at the first sign of not living up to the number. So if before you start strong-arming your next employer into that top dollar, make very sure you're worth it.

*

Promotions are never won between 8 and 5. The accomplishments that really get you noticed, that demonstrate your ability to add value at a strategic level, are rarely the ones you complete during your normal day. Many people chirp the "work smarter, not harder" mantra, but oddly enough, I've never read of Edison, Andrew Carnegie, or Steve Jobs having attributed their success to years of smart work.

*

Never take a job with a title that your next employer wouldn't recognize. The time may come when somebody offers you a job with some screwy title like "ABC Project Implementation Coordinator." Never take that job, and if you have to take it, start looking for another job. Those obscurely-titled jobs are the ones businesses offer to people who are failing in their current job, and at the next downturn, those jobs always get whacked. And once those people have to shop around a resume with their most recent experience having some quirky, one-off title, they stay unemployed a long time; employers are seldom willing to invest their time to listen to the 10-minute explanation about why this person's career took some incomprehensible detour. So in the tree of your organization's career options, stay close to the trunk.

*

You'll likely have setbacks and frustrations in your career – promotions not received, raises smaller than you expected, maybe even getting flat-out jerked around by your company. There are only two way to respond to those situations – take the road out, or stay in and take the high road.

I once worked with a guy who had been a sales leader under one boss, then taken out of that role by another boss, and returned to the role under a third. He could have given a pretty ferocious temper tantrum over that kind of treatment (and he confided in me about how he'd like to), but he just stepped into each position and did his best. His professionalism, and just plain grace in those circumstances, always impressed me.

The only road worth taking is the high road.

Playing Junior Lawyer at Unemployment Compensation Hearings

Unemployment compensation is almost as boring as workers comp, but it does have one thing going for it: Getting to play junior lawyer at appeals hearings is really fun. There is a contest with something real at stake, and success is not only a matter of how well you can make your case in the hearing (while shooting up the other side's), but also a matter of how well you've done your job up to that point.

How to represent your company at UC hearings is one of those topics that don't get a lot of attention. I'm convinced that the biggest reason is because employment lawyers, who write most all of our legal guidance, don't want wannabe schmucks like us horning in on their potential revenue. But not only are the lawyers no help, states provide little to no guidance either to claimants or employers about how best to participate in the system. So into until you start getting the hang of the process, any success you have is often something you blunder into.

Regardless of the attorneys' fear of revenue loss, representing your employer at UC hearings should be something you do yourself. Early in my career, when I was stupid and intimidated by the word "hearing," I used an attorney to represent the company on two or three occasions. I lost them all. Now, don't be too quick to conclude that the reason is because those referees looked upon the big employer and his high-powered attorney on one side of the table, and the lowly ex-employee on the other, and saw an opportunity to dispense some healthy social justice: Believe it or not, I've never lost a hearing in which the employee brought in representation. So my first piece of advice to you is don't use an attorney. You don't need the expense, and the help is, well, not that helpful.

It's true that success at appeals hearings can be, shall we say, elusive; so much so that some HR people don't bother even to attend their own hearings. That's a mistake. You won't win them all. You probably won't win most of them. But it's possible to win enough of them that it's worth your while to take your best shot at every potential claim that can be classified as willful misconduct. UC claims hit your organization's bottom line not only in the benefit payout, but also in the premium increase, which can stay with you for quite a while.

UC claims control allows you to demonstrate to your organization the financial contribution of a good progressive discipline process and thorough documentation.
What makes us all crazy about UC appeals is the referees. They are a, um, varied lot. I've been in front of UC referees who were every bit the small-minded fussbudgets as was my second grade teacher; those who seem to be spending their careers taking out their rage at failing the bar exam on employers; and those whose utter inability to follow a simple line of fact and reasoning I hope was due to new meds. I have also encountered referees who were genuinely fair-minded and consistently did their level best to apply precedent and law. I

wish I could say that describes most of them; but we takes what we gets.

I have found the most reasonable UC referees to have been those in more rural areas as opposed to cities. I think one reason I've had more success at winning appeals in those areas – well, actually, those areas are where I've had all of my success – is because those referees can get to know you a bit. If you come into their hearings well prepared, and put forth documented, well-reasoned cases grounded in the law, they come to see you're a responsible, fair-minded employer, and you start subsequent hearings with one leg up.

Like everything else in this book, don't take this as legal advice. So now that my lawyer is happy, here are what I've found to be the keys to winning UC appeals:

The first requirement is to know the law. I believe that every state allows for denial of unemployment benefits if the employee quits or is terminated for some definition of willful misconduct. So your challenge is always to show that the employee's actions met the state's definition of one of those two actions. The obvious corollary, by the way, is that the state won't deny unemployment compensation for terminations due to performance. The schlep may have cost you a fortune in shoddy work, but if that's why you fired him, he's going to cost you unemployment benefits as well – so don't even waste your time trying to pursue denial of UC benefits.

The next requirement is to know your case. There are referees who won't let people in the hearing room unless they have firsthand knowledge of the facts, let alone participate in the proceedings. As I mentioned earlier, this is why HR should be involved in the later stages of discipline for willful misconduct issues, and should at least be present at the termination. Knowing the facts firsthand, and understanding the hearing process, allows you to represent your organization with confidence and professionalism. It's important at any hearing, but doubly so if the other side brings in representation.

It's easier to plan your presentation if the ex-employee is the one who files the appeal, since in that situation he or she is trying to rebut a case you've already made. In those appeals your task is to knock down the ex-employee's reasons for the appeal. The best way to do that is to substantiate further the reasons for your actions, through additional documentation you might have and eyewitness testimony. If you're filing the appeal, think your case through clearly and carefully. Be prepared to develop whatever you state on the appeals form as your reasons, and only those reasons – piling on additional assertions at the hearing makes you look sloppy.

The notice of the appeals hearing will list the specific issues to be discussed at the hearing. Stay focused on those issues at the hearing, and don't try to bring in anything else unless it's truly germane. Referees often give ex-employees some latitude to make their cases, owing to their inexperience with the process. They pretty much never extend the same consideration to employers, so stick to what the referee decides are the issues at hand.

Identify witnesses that would help make your case and bring them with you, but I wouldn't use more than two or three tops – you don't want to look like you're ganging up on the poor little miscreant. Review their testimony beforehand and rehearse any questions you'll ask them.

Address the referee as "your honor," or as "Mr./Madam Referee."If you didn't include documentation, such as notes or relevant employer policies, you can usually ask that they be admitted into the record as well. Once everybody is sworn in, you make an opening statement. Keep yours focused on the facts, laying out what the employee did, how the employer responded, and the relevant employer policies at issue. Make sure you know the key dates – when it all started, the dates of key conversations with management, and the date of termination.

When the ex-employee has made her statement, you get to cross-examine her testimony. You want to probe inconsistencies with your testimony, and explore internal contradictions. A little well-timed mockery or sarcasm can help to undercut your opponent's credibility, but be very careful about it. In general you want to treat her calmly and professionally. Above all, don't cross-examine too much, or come across as aggressive. You're just here to see justice done, not to carve another pound of flesh from the miscreant.

Don't ask leading questions, in which you supply all the information and allow the person to answer only "yes" or "no." If the claimant brings an attorney, it's a sure bet he will try to rattle you, or sneak something by you. Keep your calm and don't be intimidated. If he yells "objection!" don't let it shake your confidence, even if it's sustained. If he tries introducing hearsay evidence, object.

When all of the testimony and cross-examining is finished, you get to make a summary. Referees will pretty much let you say anything you like. You can use this time to expound on why your opponent is a black-hearted snake, if you like; but if you do, you'll be wasting your time. This is when you should be stepping the referee through your case. You want to show him or her how the facts presented demonstrate that the employee's actions meet the state's definition of willful misconduct, or quitting, and therefore justify denial of UC benefits. You get bonus points if you can cite the relevant section of the state's UC code.

If your appeals hearing doesn't go your way, you can generally appeal the decision to the state's UC appeals board. In that step in the process, though, you can't introduce new evidence or reargue your case. All you can do is show where the referee erred in some aspect of the fact analysis or application of the law.

Now, this is the step that really does constitute a complete waste of your time. I've never prevailed in these appeals, and I don't know anyone who has. In fact, I'm convinced that the "State Unemployment Compensation Appeals Board" is not a group of UC experts, but the state's inside joke that refers to some intern in a cubicle whose job is to generate denial letters in between making photocopies.

One last tip on arguing UC appeals. Of all the terminations for what could conceivably fall under the UC code's definition of willful misconduct, the most difficult for an employer to win are those for attendance problems. However, it is doable. The trick is to show that after the suspension prior to termination (called for in your fair-minded and consistently applied progressive discipline policy), the employee committed to solve this problem forever, and then failed to follow through on his commitment. Thus, the reason for the termination was not so much the ex-employee's absence as the failure to follow through on the commitment. It doesn't always work, but it's the most successful line of argument I've found.

Information Technology

Some years back I picked up an interest in building databases, and in fact built my own HRIS. That experience has given me an appreciation for how business leaders, especially HR people, should be thinking about and applying information technology.

For all the yammering about how technology is transforming our lives and our workplaces, it's remarkable that a theory of information technology gets no attention as a management discipline. In fact, as far as I know it doesn't really exist.

I could feel your eyes glaze over upon reading the word "theory," so let me explain what I mean. For the past decade or so, HR people in manufacturing businesses have surely been exposed to the principles of lean manufacturing. Now, as a result of their own training in lean, I'll bet they could walk into almost any manufacturing operation and develop an accurate estimation of how lean the process is. They don't necessarily understand how the business makes what it makes, and they don't need to. They'd be looking for the application of 5S principles, looking at the WIP between processes, the extent to which they're applying visual management, and so on.

Now, ask any of those lean experts in HR how lean their own processes are, and the answer will likely be a blank stare, followed by a half-hearted reply like, "well, how should I know? I'm no techchie. Besides, I'm not a manufacturer."

Wrong answer! If we define manufacturing as a process by which a raw material is transformed into something of value to an end user, HR people are indeed running a manufacturing process. Their raw material is data, and the end product is information for the organization. So lean has to apply to them as well.

Unfortunately, their understanding of how lean is applied stops at the manufacturing floor. And the universally used excuse is that they don't the inner workings of the technology. Why is this ok? Chances are the Ops guy doesn't understand all the technology he's working with, either: But if he gave that excuse to the President as to why he wasn't implementing a lean process, what would be the likely reply? Hint: First word "you're," second word starts with "f."

I 'm not saying that executives should now become techno-geeks who can write code and master the more obscure features of the MS Office suite (although it would help, as would a 15-minute investment in understanding the structure of relational databases); but I am saying that they should be able to analyze their own information processes for poor design, and be able to interact productively with the IT function to create a truly lean process.

This isn't really the place to go into that topic in detail, but let me give you a few key principles that will get you pretty far in evaluating your own processes. Some of this is likely to sound pretty obvious on the page – until you realize how little it's really being applied in your business.

Anyone who has been involved in a setup reduction process knows that the biggest waste of time comes from not having all the tools needed at the beginning of the process. In HR's manufacturing processes, our analogous tool is commonly data. Whether it's in hiring, processing a status change, or just about any other HR process, the most common cause for delay is beginning the process without all of the data needed to complete it. So a well-designed process has anticipated all of the data requirements, and makes it impossible to proceed unless they are present.

Here's an example: Have you ever bought something online, and then had the company call you a week later to say they'll be happy to process your order, but they forgot to get your credit card number? If you said yes, that company should fire their IT department; because the technology makes it possible to prevent processing an order that doesn't have all the required data. In fact, the system usually won't even save a partial record.

Here's another important principle. There are three key components of an IT system: the form, the database, and the report. The form collects data, the database stores and processes the data, and the report presents the data. These components are not interchangeable. Collecting data with the same tool used to present it is generally a bad idea, because you sacrifice the advantages of either. An electronic form can be "smart," presenting the user with a narrow range of choices that reduce the opportunity for error. (As we just mentioned, it can also prevent the user from proceeding without capturing all of the information required.) Requiring it to present the data as well will almost inevitably sacrifice this capability.

One last principle; A well-designed process incorporates the knowledge of the subject matter expert, thereby eliminating the need for that person's involvement. Think about, say, an automobile assembly line: it involves dozens of people who know how to do various steps in the process, yet few, if any, actually know how to build a car. They don't have to; that knowledge is designed into the process they use. In the same way, you can buy software that will do your taxes without the involvement of a tax expert. That person's knowledge is incorporated into the tool. So you know you've got a well-designed tool when almost anyone with minimal training could use it.

I could go on, but if you evaluate your processes in light of these concepts, you may surprise yourself with what you learn, and what you can improve.

*

The most difficult thing about implementing any IT system is that, no matter how well designed is the implementation process, you are making the most fundamental decisions when you understand the least about the application. It's very possible that after six months or so of using your new system, you'll realize all the dumb choices you made regarding its configuration, and say to yourself, "Man, I'd like to just rip half of this out and start over." Your staff will hate me for saying this (mine did), but if you've come to that conclusion, you should put in the extra evenings and do it. The problems will just nag you every time you or your staffs use the system, and you won't find good workarounds for them. So if you're buying an off-the-shelf solution and laying out implementation timeline, build in some time for "re-implementation."

One aspect of HRIS data definition that often gets little consideration at implementation, and hence results in junk data later on, is reason codes. In the push to get the system up, values are often generated with no clear distinctions, and with no clear view as to what their later application might be. The result is an interminable mishmash of codes whose meanings overlap so badly, or are so inscrutable, that users assign them with no more thought than was used to create them, all of which results in data that's worth neither the time to create it nor the disk space to store it.

So if, for example, you're going to populate the values for Termination Reason, think carefully about them. What's the difference between "Left for more money" and "Dissatisfied with current pay?" And if you're going to use something like "Better Opportunity" (not that I'd recommend it because it doesn't say much), document what you mean by it so that a subsequent user will know when to assign it.

My Experience With Substance Abuse in the Workplace (Wait, That Didn't Come Out Right...)

I don't use drugs. I don't think anybody should. I hope to God my children never do. But having dealt with my share of substance abusers in the workplace, I've concluded that most of this country's approach to the issue is an utter farce.

If your organization insists on doing post-offer drug screening, at least be clear on what you're getting for them. The only value post-offer drug screening has is as an intelligence test: it keeps out the people boneheaded enough to submit specimens that are at room temperature (which kept you from hiring a dead guy!), or that fizz, or those who think you'll buy their story about having gorged themselves on poppy seed muffins the night before. I hope you're not under the illusion that you're actually keeping drug users out of your company. If you believe that, then you're telling yourself that the people who fail your random and post-accident drug screens only started using drugs after they joined your company. The truth is that many committed drug users whom you'd like to keep out of your workplace also have the brains to do many jobs for which you'd like to hire them. They are smart enough to study for the urine test, and they know how to pass it.
And I'm not convinced that, as a representative of an employer, I should care.

I've worked with many people who use drugs. In most cases, I've known that because I knew something of what these people did on their weekends, and with whom they did it. I didn't necessarily know it from their work, which in most cases was no worse than their more sober co-workers – in fact for several of them, it was often significantly better. And where an employee can meet the company's expectations for attendance, performance, and conduct, I don't know why drug use should categorically disqualify a person from employment.

I once argued this point at an employment law seminar with an attorney who was discussing the importance of drug testing. Once we had made our respective points, he went on to discuss issues around random screening, and told the group, "But if you're going to do random screening, be careful; you may get positives from employees you don't want to catch." I raised my hand again and said, "Don't you see that you just made my point?"

You might be concerned that I'm not serious about substance abuse in the workplace. The reality, though, is that nobody is really serious about it. Anybody who spends a few years in the HR chair knows for a fact that no drug ravages the workplace more thoroughly than alcohol. Potheads will miss work around weekends and holidays, and they will never run the place, but by and large they keep it together well enough to do the job – and some of them do it quite well.

Moderate boozers, on the other hand, may spend years coming in a little woozy once a week or so but able shake it off by mid-morning – until some personal crisis keeps them at the glass later and more frequently, sending them into a spectacular nosedive from which they don't pull out. And unlike most drugs, alcohol tends to reach much farther up the organization chart.

For these reasons, I tend to roll my eyes when I hear people thump the table about the need for employers to combat the scourge of drug abuse in the workplace. We all know perfectly well why the drug user is stigmatized in a way the drinker is not; because alcohol is the drug of choice for managers and executives. But which has a greater impact on a business – the stoner machinist who smashes up a $15,000 lathe, or the boozehound sales VP whose loss of a million-dollar account triggers a layoff?

Now, before you mistake me for being somehow "broad-minded," I'm going to offer you some advice that will sound pretty cold. I once had a floor supervisor and production manager come into my office to tell me that a fairly new hire who was already developing an attendance problem had just admitted to them he was a heroin user (who had passed his post-offer drug screen!) and wanted help.

"What should we do?" they asked. "We'll refer him to the EAP,"

I replied, "then we'll replace him."

"No, you don't understand," they said. "He wants to get through rehab and come back."

"I'm really glad to hear that," I said. "But we'll need to replace him."

One week after he returned from rehab the guy went back to using. Then he went through another 28-day program. Less than two weeks after he was released from that, he killed himself.

There is only one expenditure to control substance abuse that is a bigger waste of money than post-offer drug screens, and that's rehab for users of hard drugs like heroin. The recidivism rate is so pitifully high for them that it just isn't worth the investment. One of the cruel ironies of the ADA is that the requirements for employers who have employees requesting help are so pointless in these cases you're better off just managing their problems as brusquely as you ethically can. In other words, if you suspect that employee with a developing attendance or performance problem is also using, get him out the door before he has a chance to admit he has a drug problem and requires you to help them.

Culture Change

Taking on an initiative to change a company culture is not only one of the hardest things you'll ever do in your career, it's also among the riskiest. When it fails it's not only disappointing, it's usually spectacular and humiliating; but when it succeeds, it's among the most satisfying professional accomplishments you will ever enjoy. I've been part of both, and here are what I've learned are the keys to making real change and making it stick.

You often read that the prerequisite to change is top management support. That's wrong. You need top management leadership. In way too many organizations, the boss introduces a subject matter expert to the organization and tells everyone this person has the authority to lead a change initiative. It's kind of like in the Biblical book of Genesis, when the Pharaoh of Egypt gives Joseph the authority to gather up enough of the empire's grain in the good years to avert starvation in the years of famine to come.

Like in many organizations today, Pharaoh appointed his change leader and told everybody that this guy had top management support.

Now, maybe that model works when you have the ultimate power of life and death over everybody in a police state, but if you're trying to change behavior in a modern company, it's just not enough. Management can only delegate so much responsibility for creating behavior change. At the end of the day, the only way people will really get on board is when they see the people at the top taking a personal, passionate interest in what has to change. Sure, management can appoint a change leader who's also the subject matter expert, but management has to reserve key activities in the initiative for itself.

In a company I once worked for, we were trying to create a safety culture where there was virtually none. We brought in a very solid safety guy who drove most of the initiatives. But every month the business leader, the Ops guy, the safety guy, and I would do safety audits of the manufacturing area. People saw us asking their co-workers about labels on containers, or frayed extension cords still in service, or spills, and they got the message. In fact, supervisors told us that, of all the measures we took in that effort, few contributed more to our eventual success than that regular, sincere, visible effort of senior leadership.

That doesn't mean that senior management should take on all of the responsibility for change leadership itself. In fact, one of the other mistakes many organizations make is when senior leadership doesn't bring the managers and supervisors in to the effort. You have to spell out for them what you're trying to do, ask for their help, and show them how they can help you. Then give them as much encouragement and appreciation for making it happen as much as everyone else.

*

Talk about the reasons for the change that will resonate with people. We started the safety initiative, with a management goal of reducing recordable injuries by 20% in the first year. We never shared that goal with people. What, you exclaim with raised eyebrows? How can you gain people's trust if you aren't sharing management's goals with them? Well, think about it; If we'd hit that goal, how could we expect those who still got hurt that year to want to celebrate? Instead, we shared with people a goal they could get behind: to send everyone home every day in the same condition they were in when they came to work. That's a goal that focuses not on numbers, but on people. It's something people can want to work towards.

*

Pick a milestone to celebrate, but don't tell anyone until you've hit it. When we kicked off the safety initiative the business hadn't gone more than two months without a recordable injury for over three years (now you know why we needed to change the culture regarding safety). So we decided that passing that marker would be the first short-term goal. The day the business reached it, we surprised everyone with a pizza celebration and told them how proud they should be of themselves, how they have demonstrated to themselves what they can do when they decide to do something. That was another key event that supervisors later told us really helped the business turn the corner. The fact that the appreciation was unlooked for gave it all the more impact.

*

Carrots like celebrations are indispensable for creating culture change, but every now and again, so are sticks. Sure, disciplining or even firing people for breaking the rules associated with the change might send an unhealthy get-with-the-program-or-else message that stifles dissent or discussion. But do people need to get with the program, or don't they?

*

You'll have pushback, you'll have occasional flare-ups of frustration, and of cynicism. Don't get intimidated, and don't always take it at face value. Many such situations are just some people's way of finding the new boundaries of what is and what isn't now acceptable. In other cases, these are some people's way of testing your commitment to the change. They're curious to know whether, if they push, you'll cave or push back. You don't have to shove back - but do push. Keep pushing, and eventually you'll convince people that you really are committed to the change you're seeking, and they will get on board for good.

The Compassion Trap

Most of us in HR are nice people, and we want to do our jobs as nice people. I don't mean to say we want to be pushover managers; I mean we aspire to be compassionate.

When I first started in HR, I wanted to be compassionate, too. I wanted to help make sure that any company I worked for cared about people. But I can honestly say that there is no aspect of human resources management with which I have struggled more than to work out what it really means to be a "compassionate" leader.

Several years ago a company I had worked for was about to go through its first major reduction in force. It was a traumatic experience for those of us in management who had to work out who was staying and who was going. After several gut-wrenching weeks we presented the list to the company President for his approval. He saw a person on that list whose personal hardship story he knew, and for whom he felt real sympathy. He told us to take that person's name off the list. This was a decent, caring business leader, and I know that in making his decision he was following the dictates of his conscience. But he didn't know the hardship stories of many of the other people on that list – including the person who took the place of the man whom the President saved. That was a compassionate thing to do; but I never believed it was the right thing to do.

Some years later, at a different company I had worked for, an employee working overseas got drunk and wrecked a company vehicle. It was an embarrassing and costly episode for the company in the face of the customer. But in discussing the situation with the corporate legal people, I argued that the man should not be fired. This was a long time employee with valuable skills who had had an otherwise excellent record with the company. He was going through a painful divorce, and I had heard that he had been drinking heavier as a result. The guy needed a last chance agreement and mandatory substance abuse counseling, but termination would have been the wrong call. Everyone agreed, and the guy kept his job. He was very grateful, but I could never bring myself to say that that was so much the compassionate thing to do; it was just the right thing to do.

A compassionate leader will go to funerals or wakes for employees or their loved ones. He will send cards while employees are in the hospital, or maybe stop by to visit them. If he has firsthand experience with a serious personal issue – like say, substance abuse – maybe he'll share advice judiciously when he learns of an employee who could benefit from it. If that employee has accepted the advice, a compassionate leader will follow up to be sure everything has turned out ok.

What a compassionate leader will not do is use a concern for others to excuse their infractions, or treat them differently than other employees, of whose personal problems the leader is ignorant. She will not use her innate, finely-tuned moral sensibilities as an excuse to shy away from hard decisions. To do otherwise would not be compassion; that's a kind of moral self-aggrandizement that creates unworkable inconsistencies. If you're doing those things because you think they're making you a compassionate leader, stop kidding yourself. What you are calling compassion is weakness, and it will only undercut your credibility and effectiveness as a leader in the long run. If you want to do your job with compassion, do it with professionalism. When investigating possible wrongdoing, get all the facts before you come to a conclusion. When recommending disciplinary action, weigh all the appropriate factors, like precedent, policy, and the employee's previous record. Don't raise your voice to people. Praise people. Thank them. Take the time to think carefully when completing and delivering people's performance appraisals, so you can help them become as successful as they are able.

Where you see a manager treating subordinates unfairly, call the behavior out and see to it that it stops. If that sounds not so much like moral superiority as just doing your job with solid, professional leadership practices, I would agree.

One Final Heresy

I hope most of what you've been reading to this point has been ideas with which you can readily agree, that you can apply fairly soon or plan to start using. This next section, though, is likely to make you squirm a bit. In fact, if my earlier statements about pay increases didn't cause you to throw this book against the wall, this part might (just remember what I said about your Kindle).

If this isn't an issue you've thought much about before, it may be years before you agree with me, if you ever do. That's fine. Let me just say that, like everything else in this book, this part contains a lesson from experience. This lesson, however, is the result of the real world colliding with a certain long-held, fundamental orthodoxy of the modern American workplace, and you might may consider it downright heresy.

I heard this from a very smart guy very early in my career. It took me decades to see how right he was. I hope you're not as slow as me.

Chances are the President of your organization doesn't know disparate impact from a lawful order, or wage & hour exemption definitions from an implied contract, but in one aspect of employment law he's probably a self-proclaimed expert. When he tells you that someone he already doesn't like has just given him a reason to fire the bonehead, and you caution against doing that, chances are he's going to shake his head and yell, "No way, I can do what I want - *he's an at-will employee!*"

Now, it may very well be that this was the same boss who, at last month's strategic planning session, had just given an impassioned speech to the senior leadership team about how he wanted your company to be an employer of choice (a phrase you're not going to use anymore, right?), in which everybody who has earned their seat on the bus can get the support they need to go as far as they want, and be recognized and well rewarded for their efforts. And everybody nodded in solemn agreement. Yes – this is who we want to be! We want people to love this company, and we sincerely want to do the right thing by people, and cue sunshine and string music and birds chirping…

Employment at will, that sacred precept that is the bedrock of the American employment relationship, the hallowed prerogative by which we can fire a person at any time for any reason or no reason – and oh yeah, by which employees may quit at any time for no reason (the traitors). Why do business leaders who sincerely want to do what's best for their employees also fight so desperately to preserve their God-given right to be capricious jerks?

I've worked for decent business leaders who lose sleep over trying to figure out how to do the right thing by their employees. But these same decent, enlightened leaders will clutch their precious employment at will doctrine to their chests like King Midas with a ring of gold. But does their precious little treasure really reflect the aspirations they claim to espouse?

I said earlier that employees seem to view management as wearing the mask of kindness, and they're just waiting for you one day to rip that mask off and show yourselves for the evil tyrants they always expected you to be. We all want to scoff at their fear, and say, "come on, it's just lil 'ol us!" But is it any wonder they don't trust management when at every turn we've scrawled our reminders about our right to fire their sad little behinds because it's a cloudy day? And more importantly – are they right to do so? Is that really, deep down, how we'd rather do things anyway?

I'd like to think I don't – that *we* don't. But if that's true, why is it in the organization's best interest constantly to remind people that we could? If we really believe in treating people with respect, in ethical management, in holding people accountable for their performance while giving them every reasonable chance to succeed, then we should be able to live up to those principles without needing recourse to say, in effect, "screw all that – you're fired!" We should have clearly communicated expectations, managers and supervisors trained in solid disciplinary and performance management practices, and we should follow through on that training and those practices every day.

Why do they do this? I think I know why. I said earlier that employees don't trust management isn't wearing a mask. I think business leaders don't trust their organizations. They don't really understand what exposures they have under employment law, and they don't want to "accidentally" give themselves a lawsuit. So they cling to employment at will because it serves as their safety valve.

Given the costs of litigating employment matters, that's hardly an idle concern. But think back to what I said earlier about writing employment policies – that you shouldn't write them for the goofy one-off situations. There is no better example of that fault than the lengths to which employers go to protect their employment-at-will rights.

But let's face it; when every termination decision requires at least some kind of review, and many require hours of senior management discussion and in some cases legal advice, what's really left of this right? The fact is that contemporary employment law has created so many exceptions to the doctrine of employment at will that today, as a practical matter, it means next to nothing anyway.

If our bosses could be confident in these processes in their organizations, we could use this as our policy: "We can terminate people at any time. But we don't terminate anyone in this organization without a business-related reason."

Yes, that statement will make some terminations harder. But on balance, is it worth it to undermine your best aspirations as an employer in the interest of being able to boot a handful of screw-ups? Wouldn't that kind of commitment be a characteristic of the best employers? Wouldn't you rather work for that company?

HR leaders have it in their power to make that a reality. Get serious on how your company manages performance – how it formulates and communicates expectations, how it evaluates performance, and how it responds to performance problems. And then maybe someday, when you can make the boss confident that the organization is consistent and effective in performance management, you can convince him that he can stop hanging that employment at will statement over everyone's head.

I haven't gotten there yet, but I'm working on it. Really, I am. I'm confident we're going to get there, and the day I do I'll consider it among the very best of my career.

Made in the
USA
Middletown, DE